JOURNEY TO MY FATHER

Philip Congdon is a retired RAF Officer who latterly worked as a defence consultant in the Gulf before retiring to the South of France. He has been married for 36 years and has one son who works in the City of London. He is a previously published author of two books, both of which still receive PLR after 22 years. *Per Ardua Ad Astra* and *Behind The Hangar Doors*.

JOURNEY TO MY FATHER

Philip Congdon

JOURNEY TO MY FATHER

Olympia Publishers
London

www.olympiapublishers.com
OLYMPIA PAPERBACK EDITION

Copyright © Philip Congdon 2010

The right of Philip Congdon to be identified as author of
this work has been asserted in accordance with sections 77 and 78 of
the Copyright, Designs and Patents Act 1988.

All Rights Reserved

No reproduction, copy or transmission of this publication
may be made without written permission.
No paragraph of this publication may be reproduced,
copied or transmitted save with the written permission of the publisher,
or in accordance with the provisions
of the Copyright Act 1956 (as amended).

Any person who commits any unauthorised act in relation to
this publication may be liable to criminal
prosecution and civil claims for damage.

A CIP catalogue record for this title is
available from the British Library.

ISBN: 978-1-84897-123-3

First Published in 2010

Olympia Publishers
60 Cannon Street
London
EC4N 6NP

Printed in Great Britain

Dedication

This book is dedicated to David, Irene Jane, Gordon and Ronald Mitchell, the brothers and sister that I never knew.

ACKNOWLEDGEMENTS

When I first described the tale that I had uncovered to friends they said that I must write it down and what a good book it would make and probably a film. People are always kind and generous when they can be and for a long time I accepted their encouragement as politeness at not having the pants bored off them. As the information rolled in (and still is), I began documenting what I had discovered if only to relay this to the new family I had discovered in America. From this start and the positive reaction I received, I asked friends to comment on what I had written with recommendations on how I might refine, or improve my written word. For this I must first thank Mrs Pat Cocksedge who is an avid reader of the genre and provided sound advice along with Melissa Block, herself a creative writer, who kindly read my script and helped me produce a basic structure. There followed Tim Brown, a Cambridge English graduate, who helped me re-order and refocus my work away from the Thomas Hardy School of gloom which he thought I had adopted. Finally, Roger Ordish, a former BBC producer, went painstakingly through my manuscript and provided many helpful hints. English was never my forté at school and those who have received officer training in the military will know that "Service Writing", as it is called, absolutely destroys any ability in creative writing. I sincerely thank all the above from rescuing me from the dull style that a military career had instilled in me.

Research formed a huge part of the background. At the beginning, Ancestry.com was indispensable for access to census and other related documents in the UK, USA and Canada. From there I was able to obtain more specific information relating to my father's military service from the Canadian and American government archives. In particular I have to thank Miss Andrea Silva for uncovering court records of my father's indiscretions in San Diego between 1915 and 1923, Miss Sally Roberts for research relating to my father's pre-WW2 life in Plymouth along with Miss Margaret Sims of Dousland who interviewed the ostler who was present at the great fire in 1937 and kindly read my book. Mr David Coddington, a military historian, was kind enough to visit the record office at Kew where he uncovered my father's all too brief naval career by researching HMS New Zealand and its personnel and the Pacific Squadron at Esquimalt, Victoria BC, Canada. Mr and Mrs Medland of Clearbrook, Yelverton provided access to the early photograph of the Dream Tor. Maureen Mansell-Ward, lately retired from publishing, provided untold help in preparing the layout and presentation of my work and in introducing me to the modern publishing world. In the same way I must thank my niece Rachel Congdon who is herself a budding author.

Once I had uncovered the hidden family in America, albeit too late to meet any of my half-brothers and half-sister, I found that my "new" niece Irene, my eldest half-brother's daughter, could not have been more helpful, constructive and encouraging. I would like to relay special thanks to her without whose help none of this would have been possible, particularly the photographic history of the lost American family. I treasure our first meeting two years ago. In March 2007, I met my half nephew, Mark Mitchell, for the first time in Florida. He has very kindly provided copies of the letters that passed between my father and his wife during those troubled years from 1929 to 1933, which provided an insight to their relationship. The writing of this book has uncovered many unhappy memories for my eldest half-sister, Thelma. Whenever possible she has been fully supportive, but protective at the same time. She, of course, knew my father well and the sensitivities my book uncovers still hurt, but nonetheless, she has given her approval, more because she thinks that there are lessons for a modern society to learn, if they will only take the hint. My other sister, Susan, who had fleeting memories of her father has also given her approval but insisted that to her, as to Thelma, he was a loving father. I do not think that my father's love for his children was ever in doubt. Coincidence knows no boundaries. Julia Petty, an expatriate friend whom we met locally in France, has been kind enough to read through my work in fine detail as the last pair of eyes. She told me that her father had sometimes played the piano at The Ship Hotel in Brighton at the same time as my father was employed as a doorman/janitor. It's a small world.

Finally, I have my wife Mary to thank for her unstinting support and many hours spent at the computer going through endless lists of newspaper cuttings, census documents and military records on line. As a former English teacher she has also been instrumental in repairing acres of poor grammar and spelling, wondering if I would ever learn; a bit like my father really!

La Bastide d'Engras										April 2010

Contents

Foreword 17

Family Tree 19

Chapter 1 21

Chapter 2 43

Chapter 3 63

Chapter 4 83

Chapter 5 110

Chapter 6 133

Chapter 7 152

Chapter 8 174

Chapter 9 205

Chapter 10 223

Chapter 11 232

Foreword

I first wrote this book for a family I had just come to know on the other side of the Atlantic to fill a huge gap in our family history, but most of all to help us all identify where we came from. In tracing my father's life I have also come to realise that my book is in part social history of an era long gone. To an American audience my book may cause a reality check. Many will not know of the workhouse, or of its harsh, demeaning implications that remained until the 1930's, choosing instead to rely on an over glossy view of Victorian and Edwardian Britain perpetuated by Hollywood. Behind that idealised façade, and much less publicised, love triangles, split families, fraud, bankruptcy and much else besides went on as the poor, disadvantaged and plain criminals strove to survive. My father fitted in somewhere between the latter. You will be able to make up your own mind.

I was born illegitimate in a love triangle and given someone else's surname. But none of this I knew for sure until well into my second decade of life. When I became aware, more than anything else, I wanted to know who my father was and where he came from. I desperately hoped that he was a man of distinction for my own credibility. But this was the 1960's. The only way forward was to undertake the laborious process of manually checking records at Somerset House in London. But I was a serviceman often away overseas and beyond tracing what I thought might be my father's birth certificate, I made little progress. The advent of the internet changed everything. By early 2004, all was in place to begin tracing my father's life from records electronically stored on government and private record sites.

A new world of surprise, horror and dreadfulness opened to me as I began to touch the raw face of history. My emotions were cruelly teased as I learned of the pitiless past of my father's family. My paternal grandmother, Elizabeth Davida Mitchell, had died in 1898 at the age of forty-three in shabby, Victorian conditions. I doubt that she was ever actually married to my grandfather as no record could be found. Yet, she bore him eleven children. He was a simple horse and cart man from Devon called John Mitchell, she a lowly charlady. Of their eleven children, ten were to survive. My father, so I discovered, was the youngest. On the death of his mother, in company with siblings below the age of fourteen, my father was "taken in" by the workhouse the same year.

I remember nothing of my father. I was two years and five months old when he died. He left nothing, so I learned, other than debts. All I know is anecdotal (often rather guarded) from those that knew him and through reading a plethora of documentation. In his youth he was an extremely good-looking man, but sensitive about his height (5ft 6 inches). To improve his presence and stature, he wore shoes shod with steel tipped heels so that his gait was reinforced with a tread of authority. When confronting someone, he would position himself in such a way as to bar their exit, usually standing with legs apart and hands on hips. He feared no one and could converse easily in any company. His soft Devon-American accent was particularly attractive to women for whom he seemed to have an insatiable attraction. When he was with his daughters he was as soft and as endearing as a sloppy puppy. To his sons he was firm, belligerent and a harsh disciplinarian not frightened to reinforce his position by corporal punishment.

This is the story of my father's life and the unexpected way that I first found out who and more profoundly, what he was. Within this story is a cautionary tale. On the one hand it is about being aware of how important it is to know who you are and where you have come from. On the other, it exemplifies the inherent risks of parents who keep secrets from their children regarding their parentage. To be open and unashamed with your children is never going to be easy, but the repercussions of not being so may be more severe; perhaps even more so in today's liberal society when self-worth is so often the cause for concern. To live a lie is to court disaster and unhappiness. The penalty for me was to have a terrible relationship with my mother and never know that I had three half-brothers, a sister and seventeen nephews and nieces. By the time that I did know, it was too late. My mother, half-brothers and half-sister were dead.

The revelation about my father came during my military service and that is where my story begins.

Family Tree

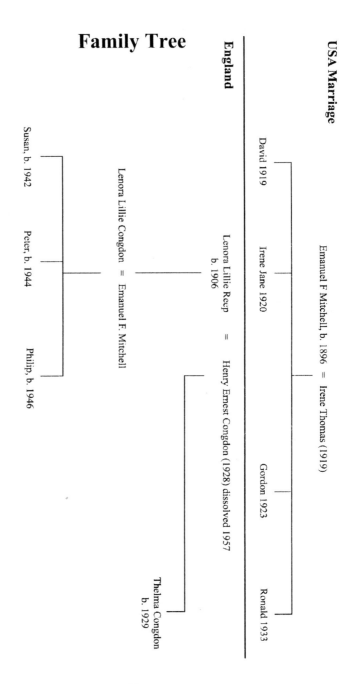

Chapter 1

The Revelation

Who am I, he asked, I don't know came the reply,
but you are sure to be somebody.
(Lewis Carroll)

"You are lying to us, why are you lying, what are you hiding?" The veins on the Wing Commander's temples stood out as he inclined his head close to mine and repeated the accusation. His breath was rank with cigarette smoke; his concentration intimidating. I was frankly terrified. The interview, if that is what you call it, seemed to stall at that moment. I was drained and lost for words. The hesitation in my reply only seemed to anger my inquisitor.

I drew in a breath slowly before speaking, "I am not lying," I repeated with equal emphasis. "It's the truth! I have told you everything I know, sir!"

If the aim of this interview had been to make me feel uncomfortable and disorientated, I had well and truly fallen into the trap. The Wing Commander seemed equally focussed on my confirming that I had consistently lied when answering his questions or, at the very least, knew more than I was prepared to admit. It looked for all to see a no win situation. I was condemned through my own ignorance. For my part, I was so tired at this juncture that it would have been a relief to agree with him, if only to bring to a halt the continual barrage and repetition of the questioning. I lowered my head instinctively to shield myself from a further onslaught, distracting my attention by focusing on the construction of the light oak office desk in front of me.

The pause went on for several seconds, or so it seemed. It was one of those occasions when silence itself becomes the whole focus of the actions being played out. From nowhere the pulse of the electric clock on the wall punctuated the moment. The minute hand jolted and grated forward as the second hand reached and then passed the twelve o'clock position. I guardedly looked up to see the Wing Commander move away, pick up a pink file from his desk and thumb through the enclosures. He was now standing in the light of the window, silhouetted by glinting dust particles that gave him an aura of enhanced authority that only served to make me feel more uncomfortable. He periodically glanced in my direction before mentally referring, I supposed, to some point or other he had underlined in the file. I had not a clue what was going through his head, let alone why the questioning had been so aggressive. Whilst the Wing Commander's attention was now taken with reviewing the situation and cross referring file enclosures, this now became the cue for the Squadron Leader to take over the questioning.

He began gently asking me about my aspirations in the Service, what courses I had undertaken and where I had served. Once more the atmosphere grew so pleasant and relaxed that I temporarily forgot where I was. We talked briefly about the parachute training school at Abingdon, which he too had experienced, and some overseas locations in the Far East. What did I think of the American involvement in Vietnam? Had I been to Singapore, did I know Butterworth in Malaya? The contrast in tone and tempo provided an unreal air to the situation. As we talked, the Wing Commander walked away from the window, sat down behind his desk, closed the file and with a deep sigh plunged it into a tray to one side of his desk where it rested half in and half out. The pink flags which had been attached to various file enclosures and were now bulging from the file, fluttered briefly as the file came to rest. The flag metaphor was as though the Cavalry had arrived, but I was its quarry.

****

At this time in my life I was a young officer serving in the RAF Regiment, stationed at the Regimental Depot at Catterick in Yorkshire. In the mid 1960's I had been commissioned into the Royal Air Force Regiment more or less straight from school. After service in Malaysia, Aden, Bahrain and Libya, I had returned to the Regimental Depot to serve as an Adjutant on what was described as a Field

Squadron. As a single fit and healthy young man the outside life, parachuting and overseas service suited me. The pay, on the other hand, made sure that the temptation to indulge in wine, women and song had to be exercised on a sliding scale related to the time of the month and the next pay cheque. More pressing were sums incurred on my Mess Bill, how much was owed to the tailor and garage bills for a 1938 Hillman Minx which seemed to have an insatiable appetite for repair.

To add more perspective, the RAF Regiment relates to the Royal Air Force in the same way that the Royal Marines relate to the Royal Navy. Not unnaturally, high standards of physical fitness were the stuff of regimental life which was based on discipline, respect and one must also say a fair amount of bullshit. In my time, the corps stood at about eighteen hundred strong and most officers knew most officers. My tour with 16 Field Squadron was coming to an end and I knew that after 2 years or more roaming the globe, a posting was due.

As I walked to work from the Officers' Mess on this particular morning, through tree lined avenues, past the red brick barrack blocks and station headquarters, a mist originating from the nearby River Swale gently lifted from the airfield. It was one of those rare and glorious mornings when the sun burns away the tired greyness, so reminiscent of British weather, to reveal the full beauty of this part of North Yorkshire. Our squadron offices were located on the airfield side of the station attached to the still camouflage-painted hangars. Catterick had been a very active fighter station during WW2 defending the key towns of the industrial North East of England. When peace came in 1945, the station closed briefly, but later re-opened as the RAF Regiment Depot thanks to its close proximity to the vast training areas on the North Yorkshire moors. For a brief moment in 1945 this airfield had its "fifteen minutes of fame" when Hollywood came to town, or to be more precise, the UK equivalent: J Arthur Rank Films. RAF Catterick was the location where the John Mills and Michael Redgrave movie, "The Way to The Stars" was filmed. This romantic tear-jerker about the Eighth US Army Air Force arriving in England in 1942 became an instant hit. It was pleasant to muse about the station's history during these early morning walks to work. However, being a fairly conscientious young officer, I tried to be at my desk ready in time for the squadron commander's arrival. This particular day was no exception. The squadron commander duly arrived and before going to his office, he put his head around my door with a jaunty, "Good morning! Any flak to warn me about?"

Life in the military can be a predictable routine, particularly when in barracks. Shortly after the squadron commander had left and following a cursory knock on my door, the orderly room corporal entered with his cheery, "Good morning sir". This ritual had changed little over my two years with the unit. He brought with him the customary heap of buff, blue and occasionally green coloured files. On top of the files was a further buff, OHMS (On Her Majesty's Service) envelope stamped 'Staff-in-Confidence' in smudged red ink, addressed to me. These sorts of envelopes arrived all the time and normally referred to personnel matters. There were one hundred and sixty men on the squadron so a single letter was no surprise. I opened the envelope without expectation. It contained the torn off portion of a teleprinter message, or signal as we called it. The message was typed in capital letters. I read the message and noted the addressees carefully:

FROM HQP&SS (SR)
COPY TO: OC AW (administration wing), S SY O (Station Security Officer). : ROUTINE
STAFF IN CONFIDENCE.
FG OFF CONGDON TO REPORT HQ 38 GP, (GP SY O) FOR DE BRIEFING 14 MAR AT 1000HRS. ACKNOWLEDGE.

My first reaction was, 'Oh shit, what have I done?' I picked up the telephone and rang through to Bob Somerset, the station security officer. He too had received a copy of the signal, but had no idea of the reason for the summons. Bob was a most amiable chap, known locally to us as the Milky Bar Kid because of his glasses and youthful complexion. Knowing the brotherhood that existed between us, I am sure he would have said something, if he had known, or at least tipped me the wink. He inquired if I had been a 'naughty boy' in his jovial way and concluded. "No, sorry, can't help you I'm afraid."

The signal had come from the RAF's Headquarters Provost and

Security Services, (Southern Region.) It was directing me to go to Headquarters 38 Group located at RAF Upavon in Wiltshire. Once there I was to report to the group security officer.

My mind quickly raced through the events of the past couple of weeks. In all honesty I could not think of a reason for this summons and, in any case, I had not long been back in the country. After I put down the telephone, I reached for a signals pad, completed all the addressees and duly acknowledged the signal in the prescribed, clipped, writing style of the day and sent it for transmission.

RAF Catterick is some distance north of Upavon which rests in rural Wiltshire two hundred miles or so south. Realising that I would need to be on my toes, bright and alert, I made the journey there the day before the meeting, spending the night in the delightful Manor House, Officers' Mess. I kidded myself that I was not really worried, but then again, it is always the not knowing that fills the dark hours with anxiety and dread. By the early hours, dread was winning by several lengths. Wishing to make a faultless impression, I had taken my best uniform and had made sure that the shine on my Oxford shoes could not be matched. I had to create the right presence! Breakfast on the morning was out of the question. The best that I could manage was a cup of tea. After this solitary, liquid repast I made my way to the rendezvous which had been identified to me by a welcoming memo left in my bedroom. By the time I was approaching the security building, the demons of doubt had taken over and I was filled with apprehension, knowing that something was amiss. What other possible reason was there for dragging me all that way? What on earth would I do if they booted me out? The RAF was my life.

Shortly before 10 am I arrived at the security building. A WRAF (Woman's Royal Air Force) corporal was waiting for me and explained that she was the personal assistant and secretary to the group security officer. She led me to an outer office and asked me to sit and wait. "The Wing Commander will not be long," she advised. We passed a few pleasantries about the weather and my journey and then she left quietly closing the door behind her. The room was quiet and still with the faint, waxy, smell of polished brown linoleum so reminiscent of military barracks. The time seemed to tick by slowly.

An electronic clock on the wall made a shuffling sound every minute when the second hand passed the 12 o'clock position. The Machiavellian ways of security officers are legendary in the military and one has to say that they are not popular amongst the rank and file. Security officers have learned to use time to their advantage as a tool of intimidation in interrogation technique. After twenty-five minutes my stomach was churning as I once more questioned myself as to what possibly could be the reason for the interview. Just then the door opened and the WRAF corporal reappeared and politely asked me to follow her. She knocked on an inner door and led me through into the 'presence'.

Two officers were seated behind a rather large light oak desk, one sitting forward of the other, the room was light, airy and a few prints of aircraft decorated the walls. A closed blue, Staff-in-Confidence file, presumably my personal file, lay to one side of the desk. A green, 'Confidential' file lay open close by with yet another pink file adjacent to it. The WRAF corporal took her leave and went to sit at the back of the office in one of those non-descript tubular stacking chairs so favoured in government offices. I heard her flip open her shorthand book as she took her position.

I saluted smartly as I entered the room. At this, both officers rose to greet me and introduced themselves, one a Wing Commander the other a Squadron Leader. They were both dressed in informal, blue shirt sleeve order. The Wing Commander directed me to sit down and set an informal tone by asking about my journey and life in the RAF Regiment. The atmosphere grew so cordial that I hesitated to think that anything might be amiss. It was explained to me that whilst one officer spoke to me the other might make notes and, oh yes, the corporal seated at the rear would record the interview. I was not to be alarmed by this. The general idea was that I was being considered for a post that involved access to secret and top secret information on a regular basis. They wanted to, 'check out a few details' with me.

So that was it. I had not done anything wrong at all. This was a sort of vetting interview. The muscles in my stomach began to ease and I could feel myself relaxing the grip on the gloves that hitherto I had clenched so tightly in my right hand. The relief was more than welcome. It was also a very clever ploy.

In the mid 60's the Cold War was at its height and the newspapers were full of 'Reds under the bed' and government ministers compromising national security by sleeping with all and sundry. A general feeling prevailed that servicemen privy to classified information were vulnerable to compromise from both sexual orientations. Stories abounded about spy rings, blackmailed homosexuals, and those who simply sold secrets for money or sex or both. Individual vetting was, therefore, part of the daily fabric of military life; nothing to worry about. I had nothing to hide. I felt relaxed and ready to answer any questions. But they were not the questions that I expected.

The interview soon got underway. The squadron leader adjusted a small green card on his desk and began. "Now tell me where were you born...? When were you born...? And what is your age... exactly?' The form of questioning was to prevent those being questioned from giving a straight yes or no answer. The idea was to encourage conversation, to get the individual talking, to open up, to relax. The straight, pressured, yes and no questions came later. In the early stages the interview covered simple facts and figures that could be easily validated. When I initially joined the RAF I had been required to complete a detailed questionnaire about my parentage on the form F Ident 177 (it's funny how some things stick in the memory). On validation of the answers I provided and their acceptance by the then Air Ministry, I was given 'Normal Vetting' or 'NV clearance'. But this cursory, security clearance was now not enough. My inquisitors clearly wanted to go much deeper than superficial information.

The questioning then turned to my parentage. My interrogators clearly had in front of them the written answers that I had earlier provided when I accepted the Queen's Shilling. As my father had died when I was a little over eighteen months old, I knew nothing of him. When I completed that documentation, I used the information provided by my mother to insert my father's personal details. She had told me that his name was Henry Ernest Congdon. He had been an osteopath in Plymouth and had died in 1948. I had no personal knowledge of him. The Wing Commander and the Squadron Leader put the same question to me repeatedly, but in several different ways. In essence, who was my father and where was he born?

No sooner had I provided the answer when the Wing Commander rapidly took over and demanded, again. "Where was your father born? When was your father born? Where did your father live?" The pace now quickened. My two inquisitors became a well honed double act. There followed question after question in quick succession where each questioner hardly allowed the other to register the answer, before the next question was aimed and fired at me. The atmosphere grew heated and intense. My questioners were hinting that perhaps my father had lived overseas. Was he in fact of foreign origin? Had he lived outside the United Kingdom with or without us? Did my mother or my father have a fluency in a foreign language? Had we undertaken European holidays as children to East Germany, Hungary or Poland? What is the name of your father? I must have been asked the name of my father at least four or five times. When did your father die? Where did he die? Where is he buried?

The questions seemed interminable. I became more and more confused and irritated. I repeated all that my mother had told me. Had I seen a death certificate? What did he die of? And so the questioning went on. Exasperation was beginning to show on the Wing Commander's face. My impatience and irritability were also becoming apparent. Just as I thought that the interview would end, the Squadron Leader started all over again. "When were you born? Where were you born? Where did you live? What is your mother's name? What was your father's name? What was your father's occupation?" The questions had been fired at me in quick succession. There was hardly time to provide anything more than a cursory answer. It was a sound tactic. It gave me no time to think. I had to offer the first thing that came into my mind. I could see that the Wing Commander was trying to trip me up verbally. But I could only provide answers from what I had been told. My mind was racing and I could now feel sweat running down my back or gathering in my armpit under the thick barathea of my dress uniform. The atmosphere had become deeply oppressive and now aggressive, with no logical end in sight. Then came that bombshell that I shall never forget.

The Wing Commander stood up, moved towards me from around the desk to position himself half sitting on the edge of his desk. He then bent towards me so close that I could smell the lingering tobacco on his shirt. He looked me straight in the eye and pronounced softly, "You are lying. Why are you lying? What are you hiding?"

****

The noise made by the pink file as it landed half in and half out of the desk tray was the cue for the tempo and direction of the interview to change once more. The Squadron Leader sat back in his chair and reached for a packet of cigarettes from the desk drawer. He flipped open the lid and before taking one himself slid the packet towards me with a more conciliatory, "smoke?"

I took a cigarette, opened my Zippo lighter, lit the cigarette and inhaled deeply. It was a comforting and satisfying sensation and a welcome reprieve in this unreal situation. The office remained silent for a short while as I continued to draw heavily on a cigarette. The Wing Commander reached for the green file, opened it carefully removing a buff OHMS envelope, stamped CONFIDENTIAL in the usual smudged, red lettering. Underneath I could see another, rather large stamp of URGENT followed by the words, SOMERSET HOUSE and my name printed in bold capitals.

If you have read Freddie Forsyth books, or have seen the film, 'Day of the Jackal', you will know that it is easy to fabricate a false identity using authentic birth certificates issued by the government. Once done and a new persona effected, it is then possible to infiltrate all sorts of government departments using this new, assumed identity. The first step is to secure an assured identity which starts with a legal birth certificate. In the 1960's the place where records of births, deaths and marriages were kept was Somerset House in central London. These records were and are today freely open to the public. By obtaining a birth certificate for an individual who died young, a false life and identity can be resurrected. The then chances of such action being discovered were remote, because there is no direct connection made between the registration of births and deaths. When the RAF security services reviewed my personal information details, on close examination, there was enough misinformation, although I never knew this, to suggest all was not well. The RAF had to be sure of my real identity.

The Wing Commander opened the envelope, removed a long slender piece of paper over printed in red lettering. "Are you familiar with your birth certificate?" the Wing Commander inquired. I nodded. "I would like you to look at this very carefully". I took the certificate from his hand, placed the lighted cigarette in an ashtray and began to read. It was my birth certificate, but not the same one my mother had given me to send to the RAF when I applied for a commission. No, this was something very different, with much more detailed information. The certificate my mother had given to me, the one that had been accepted by the RAF was what I now know to be a shortened birth certificate. This certificate only contained confirmatory information about my name, place and date of birth, my mother's name and where the birth was registered.

What I now saw was something far more comprehensive giving details of both my mother and father including their occupation and address at the time. "I want to draw your attention to the details given about your father," the Wing Commander directed, "do you recognise these details?" I examined the certificate closely. My father's details had been hand written clearly in black ink by the registrar as, 'Emanuel, Frederick Mitchell'. My mother's details were given in the next column followed by a description in a further column of my father's occupation as a 'maintenance engineer'. I read and re-read the entries. I was lost for words. Who was this man Mitchell? I then looked at the second column that gave my full name. There I saw: Philip Sidney Mitchell Congdon. I even had Mitchell in my name!

"Can you tell us anything about this man?" The Squadron Leader inquired in a gentle and mollifying tone.

"No, nothing," I replied. The beads of sweat that had run down my back were now turning cold sending psychological shivers through my body. To say that I was dumbfounded is an understatement.

"I think that you can see that we have a problem here," the Wing

Commander explained. "You tell us your father is one person, the records say something else. You say your father is dead, but the details that you have provided are for a man very much alive. What do you make of this?"

I could not explain. Once more we were plunged into silence.

"Are you who you say you are?" the Squadron Leader interjected. Now lost and completely disorientated, I had a silly and almost irresistible urge to say well actually you have caught me out, the game's up… but I thought better of it. I replied as respectfully as I could that the information that I had provided was given in all honesty. I had never seen a full birth certificate before and that my mother had never discussed my father.

The Squadron Leader methodically opened the pink file on the desk, flagged at a particular enclosure and began to read from notes. "Well, we can tell you that your father, Mr Mitchell, died in July, 1948 and was buried in a cemetery in South London under the instructions of your mother. I think that you can take it that he really was your father. There is probably more to tell, but…well…. that is not our concern. As far as we can make out, the father you described when you completed the F Ident 177, Henry Congdon, is not dead at all. In fact, he is very much alive and still living in Plymouth. But I gather from our little talk that you know nothing of him?"

"No! Nothing," I replied.

The Wing Commander now opened a blue file and began looking through copies of Form 1369; these were old annual confidential reports from past years. He said nothing for what seemed a couple of minutes, but was probably a matter several seconds. Closing the file he went on, "I think that we have stumbled on something very personal and very private in your life. You understand that when officers are being considered to handle sensitive information there can be nothing in their background that might make them vulnerable to, shall we call it, outside pressures. But most of all it is crucial that they are who they say they are. You will know from your own security training that it is possible for the Reds to assume identities and infiltrate. It's part and parcel of the cold war."

I nodded in agreement, glad that the pressure was now being taken off me.

The interview concluded as pleasantly as it started with some fatherly advice from the Wing Commander. He arose from the desk, came around to shake hands and then placing one hand on my shoulder said in a firm, but muted voice, "Look….. I suggest that you talk this matter over with your mother, there's a good chap…better to have all the skeletons out of the shadows in this game."

The shock of what I had heard was still running through my mind as I left the building to make my way to my car. It was as though I was walking in a cone of silence. Nothing registered. On arrival at my car, I unlocked the door and simply sat staring blankly out of the window, oblivious to everything. At first I felt anger and then an overwhelming, consuming tiredness. I had mentally let go from the interview and the loss of tension had left exhaustion in its place. I unbuttoned my tunic, lit another cigarette and simply ruminated on what had been said, wondering if it wasn't just a bad dream and I would wake up still in South Arabia. I suddenly felt incredibly cold. It had been a very effective interrogation that had left me almost doubting myself. Every family has skeletons in their cupboard. In my case it was a father that I had never known. I began to feel both foolish and ashamed.

****

That was the first indication that my father was not the person whom I had been led to believe he was. It was an enormous shock and it was many weeks before I could begin to think rationally. I had always known that I had a much older sister called Thelma who was 'different'. For reasons lost to me, when she first married in the late 1940s, divorced and married again in the early 50's she had been banned from the family, never to darken the doorstep again! My brother, other sister and I were very young when this happened and when mother directed that we were, 'never to make contact with her', that was clearly final. In other words, disobey at your peril! Peril was often corporal punishment dealt by a coat hanger, back of a hairbrush or a cuff around the head! They were very strong deterrents. Both my brother and sister acceded to my mother's intimidation without question. Perhaps because of my more adventurous nature and youth I found her directive harder to understand. Thelma had been a very loving older sister (17 years my senior) and I had often been left in her care when mother had other things to do. In modern parlance we had bonded. I could not desert her.

This state of affairs remained resolutely in place until I was eight or nine years old. By then Thelma had married for a second time. In a genuine desire for contact with her family she contacted my mother and asked if she could take me out for the day. Somewhat surprisingly, mother agreed. I remember a wonderful day visiting the Tower of London and going back to Thelma's flat for a tea to gladden any boy's heart. On my return home, mother once more forbade me ever to see her again. Inquisitiveness will always be the great determiner of events and my inquisitiveness about Thelma had not left me. It was perhaps a couple of years later, I cannot remember exactly, when I initiated the next contact on a sunny afternoon and knocked on the door of her house in South London. I was welcomed with open arms. On this occasion I was introduced to my niece who had not long been born. Since that date in the early 1960's, I kept clandestine contact with Thelma unknown to my sister or brother, but most of all to my mother. In all of that time, despite the rocky if not explosive relationship Thelma had with my mother, not once did she offer a word against her. On the occasions that I asked about my father, which were very few, she declined to say very much except that he had died, as my mother had indicated. Her loyalty to my mother was absolute. I remember too that one of my early expeditions was to find father's grave. In passing Thelma had told me that he was buried in Norwood Cemetery. For weeks I visited the cemetery, walking the rows of headstones, but found nothing. I thought for a long time that a much worn gravestone at the back of the cemetery might be the one. It wasn't.

****

After the interview at Upavon and having given great

consideration to the words of the Wing Commander, I seemed left with no other option but to talk to my mother. It was not an event that I cherished as at this time my mother and I were hardly on speaking terms. When we did speak, be it on the telephone or in person, a row could almost be guaranteed to ensue. Nevertheless, I telephoned her to say that I would be coming home to South London for the weekend. This seemed to please her. There were always a lot of jobs in the house that needed doing. Not unnaturally she lent on my brother and me to do the work, rather than bring someone in. In my case, my 'pièce de résistance' was the replacement of window sash cords! I had had plenty of practice. Finding the right time to broach questions to my mother was difficult, but over a mid-afternoon cup of tea, having completed the repair of one window, seemed an opportune moment. Within what seemed to be a micro second of my mentioning my father's name, my mother's face turned puce, the veins standing out on her face, her lips quivering. I had not even finished the question before rage overtook her and a tirade started. Then she was overcome with tears and shouting, which seemed almost always to be her last resort. I made my apologies and left. Had I been a more perceptive young man, I should have realised then that her reaction was worthy of greater analysis. She had been living with the fear and dread of our finding out about our father for years. She was always on a knife edge that the news might be broken to us and what would she say; what could she say, how could she rationally explain that our father's name was not the name we were called. Now I realise her anxiety. She had chosen to live a lie to protect us. As these things do, sooner or later, they back-fire and for me it had on that fateful day at RAF Station, Upavon.

Over the years that followed, I spoke to Thelma, my great Aunt and Uncle and others who might have known something about my father, but they remained resolutely silent until my mother's death in 1984. Little by little, Thelma revealed that she had known Emanuel Mitchell and that he had told her tales about Hollywood and the silent stars and that he had once been knifed in a fight in San Diego. But she had always considered them as tall stories. He also, so she said, always referred to the pavement as the 'sidewalk' – a popular American expression. As to what he did, she explained to me a little about his background in osteopathy before WW2 where he treated the great and the good of Plymouth, including the Plymouth Argyle football team. But her memories were patchy, or if you prefer deliberately vague and selective, to save me the pain of knowing more. Her final recollection of my father was on his deathbed in Dulwich Hospital, now blind and very much alone and barely fifty-two years old. Beyond these few utterances, her loyalty to my mother had been constant.

The coincident tragedy in this story has been my sister, Thelma. She had lost her father (Henry Congdon) only to become unwelcome baggage in my mother's relationship with her lover, Emanuel Mitchell. Thelma's life was one of estrangement and unhappiness resulting from the bitter, unloving relationship that she endured from her natural mother. Matters later improved, but never wholly. In the meantime, despite the financial support that Henry provided to my mother for Thelma's upbringing, he was kept from visiting or seeing his daughter. It was tragic. In cursory discussions with Thelma, I now also discovered that she was my half sister. After all that I had heard, nothing shocked me anymore. It certainly made no difference to our relationship.

My mother and I never spoke again about my father, although I suspect that she thought that I knew more than I did. She took all her secrets to her grave. From time to time in the following years my wife, Mary, made occasional attempts to find out more about my father's side of the family, but always came to a dead end. The only clue that we had was a date of birth and death and his age. In the year 2000, after many false starts, Mitchell being a very common name, the journey to find my father started. Step one was to obtain a copy of what we hoped would be his birth certificate from the records office at Southport. We were lucky.

****

I was age 60 when I first found out the details of my father's life. Thanks to the internet, genealogy sites and open government records, investigation became just a matter of conscientious research across three nations. I now know that his existence was extraordinary beyond belief. His being was the stuff of adventure, romance, seduction, destitution, riches and penury. Yet, he was just an ordinary man, from the most unforgiving of backgrounds, battling his way through life across two continents. The chapters in this book relate to the journey my father made through life. I have been lucky in as much that he had many brushes with authority resulting in a written record and even character reports about him at various stages. The military reports, US justice department and Canadian government reports have provided me with a deep insight into the father I never knew. In retracing this journey through the archives, I have also learned a lot about myself by recognising and acknowledging some of those inherited traits. It has not always been a comfortable experience.

My father's life carried the desires and aspirations of a generation of immigrants, albeit that his method of emigration was a little unconventional! He was a man sometimes ahead of his time who saw new hope, happiness and prosperity in Canada and America. There was always the American dream to inspire him. But what he could never have understood or bargained for was the cold hand of fate whose icy fingers were to hand him love, success, failure, deception, and perhaps even just plain bad luck in unequal and undeserved proportions. Most of this story is played out in the first half of the twentieth century. My father belonged to a bygone age of Victorian idealism which was later compromised by two World Wars and the social changes that they brokered. At the start of his life there was endemic class division, patriotism, philanthropy and the most appalling housing squalor which somehow all gelled together on the cushion of the Poor Law to make English rural life. By the end of his life he had seen two world wars and changes to the English social order that no one could have then predicted. The huge irony is that they were all changes from which he would have personally benefited. But that is all in the future.

Holsworthy Market Circa 1906

My father's story starts in the latter part of Queen Victoria's reign (1896). The Zulu wars had come and gone (1871-2) and unrest in South Africa precipitated the Boer War. Nevertheless, in general, life for Victoria's subjects had improved vastly over her reign with education now available to everyone. A new middle class had emerged and factories and the acres and acres of arable land ensured full national employment. These were the best of times for our nation. My father, so I now know, was the youngest son of a family of 7 brothers and 2 sisters born to a carrier (horse-and-cart man to you and me) in a sleepy Devon town called Holsworthy. Holsworthy is a hill top market town whose history goes back over several centuries to the reign of Henry II. The church and schools lie at the top of the town with the traditional market square. At the turn of the nineteenth century my father would have been familiar with the weekly general market and every three weeks there would be a special main cattle market attracting hordes of spectators as well as buyers and sellers. Around the square there would be stalls selling butter, cream, cakes, fish and every vegetable along with rabbits, hares and game birds in season. The inns would have done good business and in general children thrived on the freedom and opportunity that was then country life.

Like many English villages at the turn of the century, the fortunes of Holsworthy inhabitants went up and down in the prevailing commercial climate. With the arrival of the railway in 1879, the market greatly expanded which in turn meant more work and the release of more money into the community to build and support a wide range of shops, schools and churches. Cattle, milk and perishable goods could now be taken quickly by rail to the big towns, increasing the wealth of the farmers and traders. Holsworthy prospered. It was into this environment that on a humid, July day in 1896 my father was born. The address was modest, in fact, a rather shabby, down at heel rented cottage on North Road, but, 'one up', as his parents would say, from a previous address on Canal Road where the rats were said to be 'as big as dogs'! My father's parents were John and Elizabeth Mitchell, originally from the Exeter area of Devon. I have tried many times to locate their marriage which appears not to have been registered. But, given the time and the lack of education, perhaps they never were married. To complete their background, Elizabeth worked as a lowly cleaner or 'charlady', whilst John hauled stone and timber with a horse and cart for the builders of the ever-expanding railways.

My grandfather John found work in abundance. There was plenty of food on the family table and the rent was paid on time. In short, life was good. By the time of Emanuel's birth some of his siblings had already left home: the girls to go into service at age 14 and the boys to find local labouring jobs. That was the tradition of those times. Tragically, their third child, Mary Jane, had died in 1879. However, when fortune prevailed to provide another daughter, as happened in 1888, she was given the same name. All in all, despite the obvious poverty, the Mitchells were a close family and there was nobody quite like mother.

As in all Victorian stories tragedy strikes and this story is no different. The day-to-day life for Elizabeth was one of drudgery. When not at home attending to her husband and family, or bearing children, Elizabeth would be on her knees on cold slate floors undertaking the most menial of work. The lot of a charlady was to scrub floors, wash clothes, clean the privy, to be ever in a damp atmosphere. The repeated harshness of this work would have prematurely aged her. Her skin would have become sallow, wrinkled and blemished, her knees would be stiff and calloused and thread veins would have lined her face from exposure to harsh, coastal winds that blow on to Holsworthy in winter. Her hair now devoid of any lustre, prematurely grey and limp would be hidden under a dirty mop cap. Most telling of all would be her red chapped hands, always dry and cracked. Doubtless, her only personal comfort was a heavy shawl to protect her as she made her way from work to home. For the poor of Holsworthy, life and existence came at a price.

On January 8th 1898 Elizabeth Davida Mitchell died at home in the meanness of the North Road cottage. She had been extremely ill with pneumonia for the previous ten days. She died, so Doctor Kingdom recorded on the Death Certificate, of asthenia; simply a loss of strength. At the comparatively young age of forty-three years and after bearing ten children through a life of grind and poverty, Elizabeth had no strength to go on. Her funeral followed on January 11th. She was interred in Holsworthy churchyard. There is no stone or marker. For the poor, a simple Christian burial would suffice.

The shock, distress and loss of his wife were to follow John for the rest of his days. He never really settled, nor recovered again. Of more immediate concern was what on earth to do with four children still at home and Emanuel Frederick (my father) barely past breast-feeding? There was nothing John could do. He could not continue his work, keep home and raise five children. Whilst that may be a 21st Century solution, for a 19th century labourer with no welfare support at home, it was simply not a proposition. There was only one possible solution. John must ask the vicar and churchwarden if the town would accept responsibility for his children. In other words, he would ask for his children to be "taken in" to the workhouse.

Following Elizabeth's death in 1898, those of her children under the age of fourteen years and still residing at home were entered into Holsworthy Workhouse. John, for reasons unknown and not recorded (the workhouse records were burnt to provide school heating in the 1960's) moved to lodgings in Exeter, sixty miles away. Here he resumed his work as a jobbing carrier living in the district known as Exeter-St Thomas where he had been brought-up as a child. John had, perhaps, returned to his roots in the hope of finding solace and security. John's judgement on Holsworthy may have been that it had taken his wife. If and when he re-visited his children in the workhouse is again not recorded. But the chances are, given his work and likely small income it would have been hardly at all. Knowing my father now and if his father had been the same, I suspect that the rapport between John and other male children may not have been the closest of ties. There is a strong likelihood that John may have welcomed someone else accepting responsibility for his five children, four of whom were boys. John was to go on living a further twenty-eight years. He died in a London mental hospital at the age of seventy-six in the care of his daughter Mary. This suggests that there may have been more of a bond between John and his daughters than with his sons. If this is the case, this same trait was to show itself again in my father's relationship with his children.

Holsworthy workhouse had been built to hold a maximum of 80 inmates. The two-story building was long and rectangular rather like a barn with a small bell tower at its centre. The bell was crucial to workhouse routine to summon inmates as required, or simply awaken them to another morning. There were steps leading up to the main entrance located at its centre. Holsworthy workhouse looked just as one might imagine a Dickensian Workhouse to look; uninviting and drab. At best it was bleak and foreboding. The Guardians' boardroom lay to the right of the main entrance with the girls' day room and scullery behind. On the opposite side lay the communal dining hall, kitchens and the boys' day room. The living accommodation was at the rear. Unfortunately for Emanuel, men were on one side, women and girls the other. (In later life such boundaries to the opposite sex were, regrettably, to be a trifle to a youth with high testosterone levels). On entering the Workhouse for the first time, my father, his brothers and sisters were stripped, bathed in carbolic soap and issued with a coarse, workhouse uniform of dark blue serge.

As a matter of course, women were kept away from men including their husbands. Although this did not affect Emanuel, children were also kept away from their parents. The other inmates soon to become Emanuel's surrogate family and mentors included the destitute, unmarried mothers, imbeciles, abandoned children, prostitutes and the old who simply had no other shelter. In 1881, for example, just seventeen years before Emanuel arrived, out of a workhouse population of seventy-three, thirty-six were children of school age. Destitute children, as Dickens recognised, were the downside of Victorian life. At a reduced level, but none the less part of the workhouse fabric, there would be the itinerant tramps, journeymen and flotsam of Victorian life who had fallen on hard times and placed themselves at the sympathy of the Parish. All of these people were to become my father's immediate family.

These were the surroundings that awaited my father when he, with his brothers and sisters, was 'taken in'. As a babe in arms he would not remember his mother or his older brothers. His only reference to life, love and family harmony would be the routine of the workhouse. As we know only too well today, this was hardly the stuff on which to lay the basis of a future relationship with the opposite sex, or on which to base family life or even values in general. At first Emanuel was cared for in the nursery progressing to dormitory life as he grew-up. Religious fervour dominated the daily routine with church twice on Sundays. For those of school age, weekdays were spent at the National School in Holsworthy. On Sundays, additional lessons were given at the Wesleyan School. The routine was oppressive, always oppressive. On reaching the age of fourteen all boys would be expected to leave the workhouse to commence their adult life either being indentured to work for others, or to have found work of their own volition, which was more than unlikely. In either case the workhouse would be expected to be reimbursed for handing-on a prepared and disciplined individual to an employer. Sadly, more often than not, the placements made by the workhouse were on the basis of supplying cheap labour while the inmate had little say in what he or she was going to be pressed into doing.

This was the life that awaited my father and would shape his adolescence and mould his personality. It would also be the spur that influenced changes in his later life. In theory such beginnings had all the Victorian virtues. But reality was to be something very different. Having been brought up in the workhouse from a babe onwards he would have one major advantage over other inmates; credibility. He was 'the' workhouse child. He knew nothing else. Like the Artful Dodger in Oliver Twist, he would have assumed a natural leadership amongst his peers because of that standing. Knowledge is always the key to power in any environment. Thanks to the advice and counsel of his inmate mentors, my father would be knowledgeable and practised in every wheeze and dodge in the book of institutional life.

Notes

At the date of publication RAF Catterick is a Royal Artillery barracks and the RAF Regiment Depot has moved to RAF Honington in Norfolk. The RAF Regiment is currently serving in both Iraq and Afghanistan.

Chapter 2

Beginnings in the Workhouse

"The Workhouse should be a place of hardship, of coarse fare, of degradation and humility; it should be administered with strictness, with severity; it should be as repulsive as is consistent with humanity."
(Reverend Millman 1832)

To recognize who my father was and what motivated him I had to understand and visualise his humble beginnings. These were his workhouse years between 1898 and 1910 where the conditions under which he lived shaped the rest of his life, defined his personal values and become the basis on which he undertook relationships with his fellow man. As general background to this period, emigration to America was at its height, the Boer War came and went (1899-1901), Queen Victoria died (1901) and the new Edwardian age of decadence began and ended (1901-1910). This last point may be of some interest. Emanuel could have been more cognisant of these decadent excesses than at first might seem the case. Gossip, after all is infectious, particularly when it relates to the rich and famous. More to the point, gossip may underline the boundary between acceptable and unacceptable behaviour. But most of all it provides ideas for the impressionable and receptive mind; Emanuel's mind was certainly that.

To counter salacious gossip and prattle from the lower classes there would be the stories of derring-do from 'the Empire on which the sun never set'. At school and in church Emanuel would be told anecdotal tales to induce pride in his Nation and place of birth. There would be accounts of the Devonshire Regiment's involvement in the relief of Ladysmith during the Boer War. Moreover, a moral point and example would be made of the Devon officer (Lieutenant Masterton) who was awarded a posthumous Victoria Cross for his heroism. "Let his example be yours", the boys would be told from the pulpit. And so life went on.

There are few today who can relate to the workhouse other than it being a terrible, but necessary institution of the time. An example of how the workhouse was perceived by the public in Devonshire is illustrated by the following story. The workhouse in the town of Kingsbridge, in all respects a similar town to that of Holsworthy, was located adjacent to the main town church. The church included a square tower with a clock face on each side. Significantly, however, only three faces of the tower actually had a clock dial on it. (This remains to the present day). On the side that faced the workhouse, the dial had been deliberately blacked-out so that the inmates would be kept cruelly unaware of time. In pious, Victorian society there was nowhere more mean, base and stigmatised than the workhouse, be it Kingsbridge, Holsworthy or anywhere else; and no people more lowly than its inmates. That was the view of the prejudiced majority and of the Church of England at the turn of the 19th century.

RULES & ORDERS

TO BE OBSERVED BY
The Poor of the Parish Workhouse of Aylesbury,
IN THE COUNTY OF BUCKS.

I. That the Master and Mistress live in the House, and see that the following Rules be observed.

II. Every Person in health shall rise by six o'Clock the summer half year, and by seven the winter half year, and shall be employed in such labour as their respective age and ability will admit, and commence their work by six o'Clock in the Morning, and work till six o'Clock at Night, from Lady-day to Michaelmas; and from seven o'Clock till dark, from Michaelmas to Lady-day, allowing half an hour for breakfast, one hour for dinner, and half an hour for supper; and any one refusing to work, shall for the first offence go without their next meal, and for the second offence be reported to the Overseers, that they may otherwise be punished.

III. That all the poor in the House go to bed by eight o'Clock the summer half year, and by seven o'Clock the winter half year, and that all candles be put out by that time.

IV. That the poor shall have their provisions in a clean and wholesome manner, their breakfast by eight, their dinner at twelve, and their supper at six o'Clock; that no waste be made, nor any provisions carried away; and that Grace shall be said before and after dinner, and none may depart until Grace is said; and their dinner three times a week to be hot meat and vegetables properly cooked.

V. That the House be swept from top to bottom every morning and cleaned all over once a week, or so often as the Master and Mistress think necessary; and the windows be opened daily.

VI. That none absent themselves from the House without leave, nor stay beyond the time allowed them, on pain of losing their next meal, or of some other punishment; nor may any one be admitted into the House without leave of the Governor.

VII. Any of the poor guilty of stealing, selling their provisions or clothing, or of drunkenness, swearing, quarrelling, fighting, or in any other way disturbing the peace of the House, or of being in any way saucy or abusive to the Master or Mistress, shall be punished with the utmost severity of the law.

VIII. That all in the House who are able, and can be spared from the duties thereof, shall attend Church or some other Place of Worship twice every Sunday; and those who refuse or neglect to attend, or do not return as soon as Service is over, shall go without their next meal, or be punished in some other way, as the Overseers shall think proper.

IX. No person shall be permitted to bring spirituous liquors into the House, or smoke in any part of the premises, except the hall. Those found transgressing, shall lose their next meal, or be otherwise punished.

X. Workers shall be allowed 2d. in every shilling they earn; Cook 4d. per week; Doctor's Nurse from 1s. Washerwomen half a pint of ale each per day, and tea in the afternoon.

XI. Any of the poor acting in disobedience of the orders of the Master or Mistress, or in contempt of these Orders, shall be taken before a Magistrate, and punished as the law directs.

XII. That these Orders be placed in the hall, dinner-room, or in any other place that the Overseers may direct; and that they be read on a Sunday at dinner-time by the Master or Mistress, so that the poor may not plead ignorance of the same.

XIII. If any of the poor are found defacing or destroying these Rules, they shall be punished by being fed on bread and water only for two days.

JOHN KERSELEY FOWLER,
JASPER JACKSON,   } Churchwardens.
WILLIAM HOMEMAYER,

ROBERT READ,
JOSEPH SHAW,   } Overseers.

27th JANUARY, 1831.

Sample Workhouse Rules

Holsworthy workhouse had been built in 1853 at Trewyn, just to the north of the town. It was far enough away from the well-paved and upright district around the Church to be discreet, but within a comfortable walking distance to the market place. In 1904, a new infirmary had been added where Emanuel had weathered his childhood infections. This had been an essential addition as with so many people living in such close proximity, infection spread quickly. Opthalma, that irritating eye infection and scourge of the workhouse, was caused by dust raised in the congested living accommodation. Smallpox, chickenpox, dysentery and measles were all part of the infection gauntlet that Emanuel and his fellow inmates ran during their incarceration. In any case, child mortality during this period was high. The situation was often made worse by the poor quality of food and collective dining facilities. For many years, so his fellow inmates informed Emanuel, the use of cutlery had been denied. All food had to be eaten with the hands and all dishes were washed in cold water; each a practice that compounded any problem of contamination. How grizzly that memory remained in Emanuel's mind, sending shudders of despondency down his back when he had recall of workhouse meal times. He despaired at the chipped crockery and dull coloured wooden or metal cutlery; always, but always laboriously and tediously counted after every meal.

Holsworthy workhouse 1898

Of all the rituals, the routine of the workhouse was deeply embedded in Emanuel's memory. The Victorians were good at the management of people by strict routine. Set the routine, it was said, and you control the man. Control the man and you make sure that his every waking hour is full with no time to fritter away. Thought of that routine evoked in Emanuel recollections of his destitute past, particularly when he heard any bell ring. That toll reminded him of the workhouse bell housed in a small, latticed roof tower at the centre of the building. For him that resonant chime of a single bell announced the beginning of each day, the call to meals and the end of the day. For him, it was a daily reminder of his loss of dignity, freedom and the unwavering tedium prescribed by the Poor Law Commissioners. This tedium was, of course, an intended policy to dissuade those who might see the workhouse as an easy option.

Emanuel would awaken each morning to the ring of the bell at 6 am. At 8 pm it would toll again when all would be expected to be in bed, or at least what passed for a bed. In truth it was a canvas palliasse stuffed with straw on a rough, pine frame. Coarse flannel or shoddy blankets completed the bedding. There were no sheets. In his boys' dormitory of fifteen beds, the separation between bed spaces was only four or five feet, with a plain wicker chair placed close to each bed head on which day clothes had to be neatly piled at night. All meals were taken in the communal dining room furnished with pine tables with long benches for seating. A rather disagreeable warm, humid smell always met Emanuel's olfactory senses as he entered the room. It would cause him to gag slightly when he encountered the same smell in later life, once more reminding him of his past. He determined that it was predominantly the 'whiff' of sour milk mixed with Lysol (soap). Years of spilt milk, soup and sundry other liquids had soaked into the pine tables giving the tops a dark, brown patina. Despite the tables being scrubbed daily, often by his sisters, that decaying, never to be forgotten, fetid odour vented into the atmosphere. It was an ambience that never seemed to clear.

Emanuel's recollection of workhouse food was of boring, tasteless meals. Despite this, his nose had smelt, and his mouth salivated in response to the seductive aromas of other culinary delights. How he had been cruelly taunted by the smells of aromatic or sweetened food, or crispy bacon and sausage on the griddle, or roast beef in the oven! Of course there was other food available than the gruels and porridges so often served up. Apocryphal stories abounded of what the Master, his staff and the guardians consumed at their table. After all, all food was cooked in the same kitchen. Emanuel's sisters Louisa and Emily, who scrubbed the tables and worked as skivvies in the kitchen, had told him that there were special diets for growing children that included extra butter, milk and meat. There was another diet for nursing mothers and yet another again for the sick and infirm.

Mature Inmate uniform 1911

The staple diet that Emanuel had become used to was basic by today's standards, but nutritious none the less. For breakfast he would be given a ration that might include some bread and cheese, or furmity, a rather unappetising porridge like concoction composed of grain with honey. But it was filling. Lunch or dinner as it was described was the main meal of the day that might commence with a thick vegetable soup. The idea would always be to fill the inmate's belly as cheaply as possible. To do this, suet pudding, yeast dough and potatoes would be added in quantity. Occasionally, on high days, meat was served, but never in amounts, or with the repetition that we would recognise today. In the evening, the supper meal was kept as a cold serving of bread, cheese or potatoes. The main drink at meal times was of water or milk, often the blue, watery buttermilk left after cream had been skimmed away. Tea or coffee was an occasional beverage, never with sugar. Whatever the food provided, all of it was strictly rationed. On special occasions like a coronation, church anniversary, harvest supper or Christmas, Emanuel would remember fondly that a special menu might be planned. To the excitement of all, this may include a full roast meal, fruit tarts, or a rich fruitcake. The day would finish with community singing and a concert provided by the local Salvation Army band. Those were the days that he remembered with affection. Those were the days that drew the inmates together.

Despite the restricted diet Emanuel looked forward to meal times. It was a social high spot of the day, when he met his sisters and had a chance to gossip, albeit, conversation during the meal was overseen by a porter or nurse and kept to a minimum. But some members of staff could be more accommodating in their interpretation of 'the minimum' than others. On the other hand, high spirited or raucous behaviour would be severely dealt with by corporal punishment, a restricted diet of bread and water, or no food at all. It is not difficult to imagine that Emanuel most probably learned the hard way!

Light, always speckled with the dust thrown up from the slate floor, came into the white, lime wash interior of the main building and dining room through windows purposely placed high up on the wall. They were so high in fact that neither Emanuel nor his fellow inmates could look out. There was a kind of cruel perversity in this. Windows were designed to look out of, weren't they? Later, when he attended the Holsworthy National and Wesleyan School, he became aware of the same, cruel irony in window placement. 'Children must not be distracted by being able to look out of the window,' he was reminded.

The key to life in the workhouse was routine. It has long been accepted that people in general, but more especially children, respond positively to a set routine. It might be boring, it might be tedious, but at least everyone knew where and what they were supposed to be doing at every hour of the day. It was part of the Victorian ideal of a time for everything and everything in its place.

Workhouse Schooling

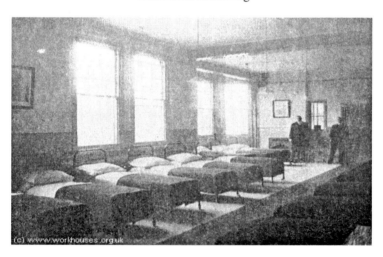

A typical dormitory Circa 1898

The routine of the workhouse continued after breakfast with work commencing at 7 am until midday. Afternoon work began at 2 pm and lasted until 6 pm. Supper was served between 6 and 7 pm. Bed followed at 8 pm. It was the same every day. In the evenings, no further light was provided after 8 pm. Candles or lamp oil was an unnecessary expense. Overall, by the standards of the time, the regime was fair, but strict. Once the responsible nurse or the Matron had completed the last inspection of the long boys' dormitory and the oak door had closed behind her, the boys would listen until her footsteps had safely receded into the distance and the matron's parlour door had clanged shut. On moonlit nights, this was the signal for Emanuel and his chums to get together and just talk as all boys love to. There were always tales to tell to while away the long nights of winter. Many of them were apocryphal about the excesses of workhouse life. A favourite tale concerned a crooked Master and his staff. These stories were handed down like folk tales. Rather like fishing stories, they grew longer in their telling. One that Emanuel remembered, described how in past times the Master, matron and porters had been able to line their pockets from hiving off items from the regular deliveries of bulk food and grain. 'Yer... 'ave e herd of... I tell e...I 'erd it from...' The tale, told in that delightful, lilting Devon brogue that rises in pitch at the end of each sentence would relay an account of adulterating the grain, stealing meat, and so on. Emanuel would listen spellbound to how men and boys at such and such workhouse were so hungry as a result of short rations that they ate the crushed bone meal that was really prepared for use as fertiliser on the fields!

There was always a grain of truth to each tale. The reality was that twenty years before, legislation had been introduced to provide better accounting controls to prevent the excesses that had given the workhouse such a bad reputation in Dickens' time. Nonetheless, the level of comfort and the wholesomeness of Emanuel's diet would be described today as sustainable, but meagre. The Holsworthy Master during Emanuel's early life was the well-respected Mr John Bries; his wife Elizabeth was the matron. She would have been a leading figure in Emanuel's childhood and would have seen him through his childhood infections. The other members of the workhouse staff included porters and assistant nurses. From an advisory point of view, the Vicar, Church Warden and Guardians provided the management committee. All the staff were appointed through the board of Guardians drawn from the parishes within the union.

The principal tasks of the workhouse staff were plain and uncomplicated: to care for and educate the children and to prepare them for an adult, Christian life, the emphasis being on "Christian". The Master exercised absolute control over the children. Emanuel had to acknowledge and accept the discipline of workhouse routine; but more to the point, the routine of a disciplined life. By necessity, the Master often repeated these tenets to his children, *"you will speak when spoken to; you must learn to respect, to honour and obey without question and to show deference to your elders and superiors. That is the pathway in this house... and no other"*. Emanuel was a bright child, unafraid and with a pleasant disposition. However, it is also clear that he was wilful and being told that he could not do something might, instead become a personal challenge that often lead to catastrophe. The problem was that more often than not, he was ill prepared for the challenges he undertook.

This facet of his character may not be surprising. Growing up in a strict, inflexible workhouse environment surrounded by thirty or so children, all of different ages and abilities would have been challenging. In this environment there had to be an element of natural selection, and the Darwinian concept of "survival of the fittest." Emanuel clearly did survive and became a recognised character and leader into the bargain. As a result of his antics and extravert behaviour his peers gave him the nickname of "Jumbo". He was certainly not big for his age so the only assumption is that it was his impetuousness and bravado that brought him to the fore.

Quite what happened to Emanuel's eight brothers and sisters: Frederick, Bessie, George, William, Mary-Jane, John, Louisa, and Emily is not fully known. After their mother Elizabeth's death in 1898, her four children under the age of fourteen, John, Louisa, Emily and Emanuel, were admitted into the workhouse. It is unclear how much contact the children had with each other, but we can be sure that Louisa and Emily looked out for Emanuel and were probably given many of the simple care and feeding jobs during his infancy. Sadly, the Holsworthy workhouse records have not survived so there is no detail. The only way to follow the children has been to look at the census documents for 1901. From these records we know that the eldest son, Frederick, got married and worked as a farm labourer in the local village of Pyworthy. Mary Jane became a servant to a farmer called Thomas Yeo and William went off to be a teamster for farmer William Jones of Lakes, close to Holsworthy.

I can only assume that Emanuel's older siblings who lived in the Holsworthy area visited Emanuel as their time and finances permitted. The then working week was six to six and a half days, so it may not have been often. It is, however, easy to imagine John, later Louisa or Emily bringing gifts of food, sweets or underclothing to soften irritation from Emanuel's rough serge, workhouse uniform. After all, they all knew the deprivations and what life in the workhouse was like. The delight on Emanuel's face must have been a rare moment of true happiness as his brother or sisters came into view on a sunny, Sunday afternoon. Perhaps they would take him for a walk in Victoria Park, or down to see the great seven arch railway viaduct that straddled the leat, a local name for a manmade water course. How exciting it was for a small boy to watch the steam trains make their way over the viaduct and to listen to the shrill cry of the whistle. Perhaps Louisa had one of those farthing sweets that made a little boy's mouth water? But most of all this was the time when they could exchange information on how father was, what Bessie was doing and did Frederick enjoy his new job and oh yes have you heard from George? At that age, they would have needed each other to keep their identity and self-respect.

The need for employment coupled with cheap railway travel would inevitably split the Mitchell family. Mary went to Stratford upon Avon to work and later to marry. Bessie went to Southampton to be a vegetable maid, met and married a male house servant and then went onward to Long Island in America. The family bonds were fracturing through the necessity to find work. More and more, Emanuel would be left on his own. More and more Emanuel would be fashioned and moulded by the strictures of the workhouse as family influence waned. For education, Emanuel attended the National school in Holsworthy. Here he soon recognised many differences between himself and other pupils. He would have perceived how poor his rough, blue-serge workhouse uniform appeared compared with the finer cottons and crinolines of other children. Perhaps they even spoke differently, albeit the articulation would be in a strong Devon brogue, but their grammar more conforming than his. Photographs taken at the Wesleyan School he attended on Sundays show just how smart, in comparison, the other boys looked in their Eton collared uniforms. Together with his workhouse chum Bill McCarthy (seen next to him on the photograph) he would have been more than conscious, perhaps even sensitive to the disparity and stigma attached to their workhouse origins and dress. Of all people, children can be the cruellest to each other!

Meal time in the Workhouse

Everything Emanuel experienced at school would emphasise difference. Nowhere was this more evident than in the comparison with the town children from conventional families. It was not just their dress and the way that they spoke that was different; it was also in their presence, how they interacted with each other, what they ate and what they valued. Emanuel could not help but become increasingly aware of what we now describe as disadvantage and deprivation, although I doubt that he thought of it in those terms. Deep down would be a natural desire within him to be like them and to have and to enjoy what they had. But that wasn't possible. He had to wrestle with the fact that for reasons he could not comprehend they were luckier than him. I do not think that he was ever to resolve that conundrum. As he matured in the workhouse his greatest difficulty would lie in social skills of making and keeping relationships. There was no sophistication and little feeling to his early life. Certainly none that highlighted the respect and reverence a loving father gives to his wife and children. He had no idea of how real love and affection were shown, other perhaps than listening to crude sex talk he heard in the corridors. On the other hand, he quickly grasped how sympathetic words were a route to achieving more affection.

The regime in the workhouse had been easy for Emanuel to accept. Quite simply, he knew no different. He was a babe in arms when he was admitted. He spoke his first words, made his first steps and cut his first teeth in the arms of the nurses and his sisters, all inside the workhouse. Because of this bonding his relationship with the Master, his wife and the nurses was, most probably, one of mild affection, perhaps even favouritism. Although he was of diminutive stature (the workhouse diet hardly encouraged physical development- his final height was 5ft 7") his impact may have been more profound. His nickname of 'Jumbo' again suggests peer acceptance and standing. His credibility amongst his peers was that he was, 'the workhouse boy'.

In 1908, Emily, the last of Emanuel's sisters, left the workhouse to go into service locally. She had reached the age of fourteen. In May 1910, Edward VII died and the brief but much acclaimed Edwardian era came to an end. On July 22nd 1910, Emanuel reached his fourteenth birthday. It was now time for him to leave the workhouse, and enter the new Georgian age as an adult.

A group of younger Wesleyan School children photographed circa 1910. From l-r: BACK ROW: teacher unknown, ? Petherick, W Tucker, 'Jumbo' Mitchell, W McCarthey, Fred Balsdon, ? Hicks and ? Balsdon. SECOND ROW: A Manning, R Yeo, ? Gliddon, ? Tucker, J Parker, ? Batten and ? Hicks. THIRD ROW: A King, N Vanstone, M Vanstone, C Bennett, P Bennett, ? Gilbert, unknown and unknown. FRONT ROW: W King, unknown, unknown, ? Coombe, unknown, A Petherick, unknown and C Yeo.

In 1910 as Emanuel entered adult life the world changed again; the Union of South Africa was established with its capital at Pretoria; in Portugal they dispensed with their monarchy; in Mexico a very bloody revolution began; in America William Taft was the president, the Boy Scouts of America were formed and Thomas Edison continued his scientific investigations into the transmission of sound and invented the kinetophone, a machine that made "talkies" for the film industry a reality. (However, it was to be another fourteen years before an acceptable sound system could be refined for the cinema.) In England, the new king, George V, was altogether a more gentle soul in comparison with his flamboyant father. Great Britain was at the height of its colonial power with a King, Emperor of India and an Empire on which the sun never set. It was now time for Emanuel to move on from the workhouse. Despite his humble beginnings, the National School would have filled Emanuel's mind and fuelled his imagination with the wonders and riches of the Empire. As he could not see out of the school window, an easy distraction was to daydream, looking at the countries coloured pink on the waxed-linen world map that hung in each classroom. He particularly liked the pen and ink illustrations of scenes from the Empire that adorned each map corner. When the teacher's eyes were averted he would occasionally allow himself to be transported to those far off places in moments of fantasy. He was certainly a dreamer. But reality, not fantasy was now facing him.

It had been long customary for farmers, businessmen, estate managers or apprentice masters to maintain contact with the workhouse. There was always a demand for good workers, especially young, impressionable well-disciplined boys and girls from the workhouse. The truth of the matter, however, was more to do with economics; young labour was cheap labour; cheap labour meant more profit. It also has to be said that indenturing inmates provided a useful income to the workhouse. By 1910, the many opportunities for work in Holsworthy, earlier brought by the arrival of the railway, had dried-up. There were now visible signs of unemployment with all its tragedies. As much as the railway brought employment, the paradox now was that it provided the means for families to leave if they were brave enough to take up the challenge. Where to go was not difficult to decide. Newspapers heralded the possibilities of free land for homesteading in the Dominions or the United States. It was said that skilled artisans, wheelwrights, carpenters, plumbers and bricklayers could earn their fortune and that there was ranch-work in plenty for farm workers. The only investment required was an £8 ticket on one of those huge, White Star Line steam ships that plied the oceans from Liverpool or Southampton. Many Holsworthy families accepted this challenge and were to find a new life in the USA or Dominions.

Talk of migrant activity to escape poverty and the workhouse would have spread around the town like wildfire. In some instances the workhouse union would have sponsored emigration to reduce numbers, particularly amongst young orphans. Some Dominions even asked for children under Christian welfare and resettlement schemes. Emanuel could not have helped but soak up the buzz of conversation and general tittle-tattle that he heard in the market-square or amongst workhouse inmates. Was it to be America, South Africa or perhaps that great farming land, New Zealand? Even then, in his fourteenth year, he may have harboured ideas of quitting Holsworthy. But the lack of money to buy that £8 ticket would have made this impossible. No, that would have to wait. He must bide his time. In any case the workhouse had already indentured him to work on a farm.

The dye would now be cast which would determine Emanuel's immediate future following his fourteenth birthday. Like it or not, he would be indentured to a farmer. There is always a reason for everything. In this case, it appears on first sight that Farmer Druford's lack of male offspring brought him to the workhouse master to enquire about *"taking-on a boy"*. Although, according to the 1911 census he had two spinster daughters: Edith, 29 years and Florence 18 years, Thomas needed young strong hands to undertake farm work. There was also the fact that Thomas Druford was now aged 60 and his wife Elizabeth aged 64. One can almost sense an urgency to introduce young, male blood on to the farm. The census reports that Emanuel became a farm servant at the very isolated North Heale Farm, High Bickington to join two other male employees in their twenties who looked after the farm horses. Emanuel's specific responsibility was to be a "cow boy", although he would be expected to help with all aspects of farm work as the seasons changed. High Bickington was about 30 miles from Holsworthy, but easily connected by rail via Umberleigh.

For the next eighteen months or so Emanuel learned the skills of a farm labourer. The life would have been bleak and much would be expected of him. This was a life of horses providing the motive power and long days of manual work with the 'boy' doing all the lowliest of jobs; nearly always involving shovelling dung! Looking on the brighter side, from time to time he would hand milk the heavy boned and thickset South Devon cows, carry milk and maybe turn the butter churn, although this was mainly work for the women. In the spring there was always ploughing to be done and so his life unfolded in the quiet Devon countryside completing varying farm work through the seasons. For a while the bucolic life may have suited, but it was never likely to sustain his intellectual needs. Each season came with a new challenge on the land. Ploughing in autumn or spring was followed by harrowing the ground to break down the soil ready to sow the corn or in the new parlance of the time, to drill it. In early summer there would be the hay harvest when the reaper and binder would mow the long grass in ever decreasing squares cuts around the field. As time went on the work would have become more and more tedious and irksome.

Mid to late summer was the occasion for general maintenance, repairing the barn and fences and ensuring the fresh water supply was unhindered. In late August or early September it was time for the reaper and binder to cut the corn. The method of drying by placing the wheat or barley sheaves into stooks was always the same. Everyone on the farm helped in this labour intensive, back breaking work. The carefully dried stooks had then to be thrown up to the rick by pitchfork, ready for threshing. After threshing, the heavy grain sacks had to be loaded onto a cart and then unloaded into the barn. Finally, the season closed with the re-fertilisation of the fields by spreading acres of dung by hand and pitchfork. By the end of corn harvest, Emanuel's arms and legs would ache the ache of the dammed. There was now only winter with its relentless cold and wet to look forward to and then, after Christmas, the cycle of farm life started again. Having seen the cycle of seasons Emanuel may now have asked himself; was this what he wanted for the rest of his life? It was the same question that I was to ask myself fifty three years later when I worked on a dairy farm close to Tavistock.

On Sundays after church, in the market square and at harvest suppers, much of the local gossip would have been about former farm labourers who had left Holsworthy to seek a new life in the colonies. Everyone loved the rags to riches stories because they were the only tales of hope for the future. Could this be the solution that Emanuel was looking for? At the same events he would have also heard whispered, subdued stories. Some of these related to failure, others regarding the perils of travel, particularly the loss of several local lives when RMS Titanic sank in April 1912. On hearing this, Emanuel's devil-may-care attitude would have reasoned that the likelihood of another, similar disaster was remote. In any case, a sinking ship or icebergs were not the problem of his present predicament; his dilemma remained finding the necessary finance for the venture. How on earth was he to raise the £8 it would cost to buy the needed steam ticket on wages of five bob a week? (US 50c)

Fate was now to take a hand in Emanuel's life. In the early years of the new century an arms race began between England and Germany. The 'weapon of mass destruction' of the time was the Dreadnought. This was an impressive class of battleship boasting the heaviest firepower then available. The political question in contention was who would dominate the sea-lanes of the world: the Koenig's Marine of Germany, or the Royal Navy (RN)? British politicians, inspired by the legendary Admiral, Jacky Fisher, were in no doubt that Britannia must rule the waves to protect her trade routes to India and her colonies. The consequence of this decision was that in the years 1904 to 1914, His Majesty's navy was to undergo an unprecedented expansion. On the one side, several new Dreadnought battleships were commissioned. On the other, since each battleship would require over a thousand men, an immense number of new sailors were needed to be recruited. The best way of finding this manpower was for the Royal Navy to form recruiting teams to scour the towns of England looking for 'likely lads' on market days. The inducement would be a promise of exciting overseas service in the Empire, good rates of pay and the chance to cruise the oceans of the world. Devon, after all, had a wonderful reputation for providing sailors including Drake, Frobisher and Raleigh. And wasn't Devonport, one of the nations most important Naval dockyards, only just an hour or so by train from Holsworthy?

On a spring day in 1912 a Royal Navy recruiting team ventured to Holsworthy on market day looking for new recruits. One can imagine them arriving at the station and then making their way almost swaggering across to the market square to set up their stall. The sailors would present themselves in their crisp bell-bottom trousers, bleached white caps and lanyards, their tanned or bearded faces oozing testosterone and manhood to the impressionable youngsters. They would tell tales of far off places, always bathed in sunshine, and the ladies; oh how all the ladies loved a sailor? In truth, Emanuel had nothing to lose and all to gain.

"Come my lad, your King and Country need you, sign on and see the world and have your first tot of rum." Here was an opportunity of a lifetime to escape the mediocrity of a moribund, tedious pastoral life for true adventure and excitement. But the best part was there was nothing to pay! In fact, he would be paid a wage more than a farm labourer with board and lodgings thrown in, plus a crisp, smart new uniform. The decision was made; he would sign on and become 'a jolly Jack Tar,' or 'blue jacket' as they were known in Plymouth and Devonport.

For whatever reason Emanuel now wished to make himself appear to the Naval authorities two years older than he was. This was most likely a matter of age relating to higher starting pay. It was also Emanuel embarking on an early wheeze to squeeze as much pay as he could out of the opportunity that faced him. In hindsight, of course, at that time there were no birth certificates or official documentation for the authorities to check. Contract was by word of mouth. Emanuel quickly realised that all he had to do was bullshit the recruiters. In any case, the Royal Navy, so his chums told him, would accept whatever he wrote down or said. They were not interested in the nif naf, only in strong willing recruits. (Was this the perpetuation of the Nelson touch in turning a blind eye?) At the flick of his wrist, Emanuel now gave his age as two years older, signed on and was accepted into the Royal Navy, now giving his date of birth as 1894. This was the first of many occasions when his disregard for fact falsified government documents.

In mid August 1912, just after his sixteenth birthday, my father was notified to report to His Majesty's Royal Navy Barracks, Devonport. The business of his earlier indenture by the workhouse to the farmer remains unclear. An indenture was normally for three or four years? It is possible that his new master may have released him. But knowing my father as I now do, I believe that there is a strong suspicion that Emanuel deserted his employer, to run away to sea following in the best traditions of 'Boy's Own' adventures shouting "bollocks to you" as he left. But more seriously, his behaviour displayed an early disregard for authority and the rule of law which was to follow him all of his life. His mentors at the workhouse had been effective.

****

Notes:

The Holsworthy workhouse closed in 1930, but continued to provide poor relief re-named as the Public Assistance Institution. It then became a hospital for the elderly, sick and infirm before eventually being sold and converted into flats. The building remains today. The town railway station closed in October 1966 although much still remains of the old bridges and viaducts. The house on North Road is still there but very much improved having been joined to the cottage next door. Any reference to Farmer Druford noted on the 1911 census and his farm at Nort Heael has now disappeared.

Chapter 3

Navy Days

*"We sail the ocean blue and the saucy ship's a beauty
We are sober men and true, and attentive to our duty"*
(Gilbert & Sullivan HMS Pinafore)

The eight-fifteen from Holsworthy, ('change at Exeter St David's for Plymouth and Devonport') was on time as usual. Emanuel had mustered what few possessions he had (and they were very few) into a second hand and much used carpet finish, Gladstone bag. The ticket clerk exchanged his railway warrant for a ticket and wished him good luck; he was sure, he said that the Navy was the life for a young man. The eight-fifteen had come down from Bude and was already standing at the station, steam slowly rising from the engine as it waited patiently while full churns of milk were being loaded into the guard's wagon.

Emanuel walked down the platform towards the rear of the train until he saw the number three painted in black on the brown and cream coloured carriage door. The train was in the livery of the Great Western Railway or as it had become known, 'God's Wonderful Railway'. Emanuel took one backward glance, opened the carriage door and mounted the train. The wooden seats in the third class carriage had been smoothed by countless serge trouser behinds, leaving a rich patina. Everything looked inviting, Emanuel thought, as he seated himself adjacent to a window, slipping the Gladstone bag up on the rack above him. The carriage was sparsely populated and everyone seemed to keep very much to themselves; a very British trait. The stationmaster closed the carriage door behind him with a confident clunk. At the rear of the coach, the train guard checked his fob watch and then raised his green flag toward the engine driver, blowing his whistle at the same time. The train gave a sudden shudder, the guard mounted the wagon and the train was off. Emanuel's first big adventure in life was under way. He had not long turned sixteen and the world was his oyster.

The Devon countryside is amongst the prettiest in England, with rolling hills, velvet green valleys spotted by villages with cottage roofs decked in thatch. Emanuel marvelled at just how pretty it looked. Some cornfields had already been cut with the stooks regularly sited to form a grid pattern over the field. His thoughts returned briefly to the harvest he had just left and the good wishes expressed by all for his future. The good weather of August 1912 extended into September and the sun-dappled journey provided Emanuel with an enormous feeling of contentment. What's more, there was the expectation of excitement to come. The gentle rhythmic motion of the train soon proved soporific, and Emanuel allowed himself to daydream, but he was quickly brought back to reality on hearing the high-pitched whistle that sounded whenever the train entered a tunnel or crossed a road. At Exeter Central, he changed trains to join the Southern Railway's London train from Waterloo. This line snaked across the edge of Dartmoor over beautiful stone viaducts on to Plymouth and Devonport. At Tavistock South the train halted for some time to allow passengers from other connections to join the train. Emanuel looked out of the window and noticed a fingerboard on the opposite platform which read, 'via Yelverton for Dousland, Burrator and Princetown'. Emanuel was amused by the word 'Dousland' What is or was a Dous, he mused to himself?

This had been Emanuel's first journey by rail and he was enjoying every moment. As the train approached Plymouth the line followed the estuary and Emanuel had his first glimpse of the port city. The estuary was full of boats of every kind from small single mast fishing boats to steam driven launches and cargo ships. Further out to sea he observed the silhouettes of bigger, commercial and naval vessels riding on the tide. A cold wave came over him as he realised that there was no turning back, but it quickly passed off in the excitement of expectation to come.

The distance from Plymouth, North Road station to Devonport was just a few minutes. When the train stopped Emanuel gathered his few belongings and made his way out of the station. At the station entrance he stopped momentarily to find his bearings and to observe the ebb and flow of life. Devonport was a busy commercial and naval dockyard surrounded by myriad streets of two up two down terraced houses. Horse drawn transports plied the roads and everywhere looked as busy as Holsworthy on market day. Emanuel, liking the buzz that he now felt, pulled his shoulders back, picked up his bag and made off down the hill to the barracks. The Royal Naval Barracks, known as HMS Vivid, were located ten minutes' walk away down the hill, behind the grey, stone dockyard wall. These were relatively new barracks completed in the 1890's to accommodate five thousand men. Emanuel's admittance into the Royal Navy had coincided with an unprecedented expansion of the Service. The Admiralty, lead by Admiral Jacky Fisher had realised that if seamen were to be retained to man the new Dreadnoughts, their conditions of service had to be greatly improved. Not least of all, there was a need to provide modern, sanitary and comfortable barrack accommodation, good food and effective training facilities. The days of pressing men into service were over as were the days when sailors signed on for just the voyage. The navy now offered a contracted career of twelve years.

As he walked down the hill Emanuel saw a vast expanse of tall, neatly positioned grey stone buildings clustered around the head of Keyham creek. The scale and vastness of what he saw deeply impressed him. It was a lot for a sixteen-year-old country bumpkin to take in. He stopped again, increasingly in wonderment. Parties of neatly dressed sailors were to be seen, not walking, but marching between buildings, their arms and legs swinging in a swaggering, rolling gait, or was it because their flared bell bottomed trousers gave that effect? Emanuel mused over this phenomenon. Sometimes they were in twos, other times in ranks of ten or twenty like the Militia when it paraded on Holsworthy market square. The first thing that came into Emanuel's sight as he approached the dockyard gate was the imposing, clock tower which soared above the other buildings in what today we would call an Italianate style. The bell chimed eleven o'clock as he crossed the impressive gate threshold and made his way to the guardroom. Some things never change he thought to himself, it's just like the bloody workhouse, bells, bells, bells.

On September 2nd, 1912, my father signed-on in the Royal Navy for twelve years service and duly received the King's shilling. The next step was for the Royal Navy to change my father from a country yokel into a man of the sea. Naval recruit training was not intended to be anything other than an accelerated learning programme into manhood and obedience; skills training came later. Mould the man and we can make the sailor was an adage of the day. Once those two objectives were achieved, the individual would be malleable enough to train in the necessary nautical skills. Emanuel's initial training lasted from September 1912 until February 1913. The descriptive term 'rank' is not really applicable amongst seamen who use an older word called 'rating'. This word derives from the old sea going idea that a seaman would be paid a rate of pay for the skills that he undertook. Thus the more proficient he was, the higher his rate or rank.

HMS Vivid Plymouth 1912

Starting at the bottom of the ladder for an immature sixteen year old posing as an eighteen year old would have been both physically and mentally challenging. Much of the basic training consisted of hard almost brutish, physical effort. Many of the ships of the time relied in part on sail power as well as steam. The effort and skill needed to climb the mast heads and unfurl and later furl the heavy canvas, sometimes in adverse weather, required hard physical practice day after day. If he had thought carrying grain sacks was heavy work, dealing with billowing canvas was the stuff of nightmares. There was also close order drill, inspections every day and a whole new nautical language to learn. Days were spent in general seamanship training, from rigging a hammock to darning socks and of course all of those knots had to be learned. Emanuel would be ceaselessly bullied by the petty officer regarding the stowing of his hammock. "This is your life saver" the petty officer would bellow, 'it must be stowed and rolled so tightly that if we are ordered in action to abandon ship, it will become your life preserver!' This was just another thing to learn along with putting white Blanco on webbing equipment (gaiters and belts), washing and pressing the uniform, whitening lanyards, bulling boots until they had a mirror finish and folding those darn bell bottom trousers to exact creases that the Petty Officer would check. The most unforgettable item of a sailor's personal equipment was the 'ditty box' which contained those small personal possessions so treasured by sailors and allowed onboard.

For the first two months there were no weekend rest days. Every day was a training day with a routine laid down by the Master at Arms and overseen by Petty Officers. The ship was organised into Divisions with its own complement of officers who were rarely seen other than at inspections and musters or 'divisions'. When not working on training or repeating the various drills, there were the domestic tasks to be done, laundry duty in the purpose built facility or more often galley duties. After two months, Emanuel and his chums were allowed on their first 'liberty boat ashore'. The Master at Arms had earlier said to them, when the question had been posed, that they would not be allowed ashore until they could conduct themselves as efficient, smart members of His Majesty's Navy! Seemingly, the time was about to come.

Nothing is as simple as it first seems, and so it was in the King's Navy. Metaphorical liberty boats were allowed to leave HMS Vivid, (as at sea) at specific times. The fact that Vivid was a shore establishment made no difference. All names would be taken of those going ashore (the liberty men) and the time noted, with the advice that the returning liberty boat would be at such and such an hour. Failure to return on time was described as someone 'cast adrift'. The penalty for this heinous crime would be 'on Captain's orders' which meant a disciplinary hearing usually resulting in a fine or restricted privileges or at worse a period in the brig (cells), if found guilty or proven.

Emanuel would have been in high spirits for his first venture ashore resplendent in his new uniform. It would also be his first trip to the big, 'bad' city of Plymouth. During the nights before, after 'pipe down' had been announced by the petty officer and the lights extinguished, the young sailors, swaying gently in their hammocks would endlessly talk about what they were going to do on their first run ashore. There was just so much to see and do. Plymouth had been a key naval port since the days of Drake. The years had customised the city to the needs of sailors; particularly those personal needs for single men after returning from a long cruise. There were many favourite haunts, particularly along Union Street which had gained a reputation for the key entertainments, those typically enjoyed by sailors ashore! Union Street was also the main thoroughfare to Plymouth from Devonport and Stonehouse (where the Royal Marines had their barracks), into town. Hansom Cabs did a brisk trade and the shore patrol was never far away to keep order and discipline when drink had got the better of the 'liberty men'.

Union Street 1912

When the fleet was in port, a Saturday night 'down Union Street' was something to be seen. A capital ship of those times could have a crew of over a thousand hands, organised into three watches, all of whom would be entitled to liberty in port at one time or another. When the fleet was in with 4 or 5 capital ships, Union Street would be teeming with thousands of 'blue jackets' eager to enjoy themselves. And that is what Union Street provided, a myriad of public houses, restaurants and, of course, brothels.

At the heart of Union Street was the Palace Theatre with its distinctive dark maroon tiled facade. Here continuous revues were performed twice over most evenings. 'Queenie', as she was called had a box in the theatre and held court surrounded by well dressed gentlemen more often in company with other pretty young ladies. Queenie was a euphemism for the self-styled queen of the prostitutes, a popular figure of the time. There was a great deal of folklore about this lady of the night which Emanuel naturally found fascinating, since he was approaching sexual maturity. Over his first pint of mild ale in one of the long bar pubs, the conversation could not help but turn to the fairer sex. Emanuel would listen goggle-eyed as an old tar beguiled him with fantasy stories, 'as long as Jacobs's ladder', about the lavish brothel that Queenie owned in what purported to be a respectable, nearby hotel. 'These weren't hags', he was advised in a tone leaning towards admiration, 'but young ladies of the softest disposition, skin as white as snow and smelling of roses and who could turn an evening into ecstasy; and a boy into a man'. Emanuel was not one to miss a chance. He parted with the requisite sum to confirm and validate his manhood. He was to find this experience was to give him a taste, if that is not an awful pun, for sexual excitement. As Secretary of State Kissinger was later to remark, "power is the greatest aphrodisiac." Emanuel was soon to find that his personal power and charisma was all that was needed in the chemistry of attraction. Nevertheless, he was lucky that his encounter had no repercussions. Many a sailor had to visit the medical officer under the pretence that *'my willy has a cold with the sniffles*!' It was then the case that sailors who contracted Venereal Disease (VD) would lose their pay until cured and returned to duty. The mercury cure then on offer was eye wateringly painful, let alone the months without pay.

Not surprisingly, vice was rife in Plymouth to provide for the needs of countless sailors of all nationalities who visited the port. The two aspects of prostitution and drink melted together in this part of Plymouth which also had the reputation of being rough and unforgiving for individuals who transgressed its local customs. For those who sought something more akin to home life, at the bottom of Albert Road near Devonport Dockyard was 'The Royal Sailors Rest', otherwise known as Aggie Weston's. Aggie Weston was one of those Victorian icons who wanted to provide off duty sailors and marines with something better than beer and prostitutes. This charitable lady opened a restaurant for sailors in 1873. Over the years to 1914 it gradually became an internationally recognised institution where sailors could relax, read the newspapers and enjoy a good, cheap meal. The other side of Emanuel's personality desired academic stimulation. He enjoyed reading and learning and took pride in the practical skills he acquired. It comes as no surprise that during his time at HMS Vivid, having absorbed the Chief Petty Officer's talk on the perils of VD followed by graphic descriptions of the horrendously painful treatment, Emanuel would opt to go to the reading room at Aggie's in preference to the seduction of Union Street. In any case, his silver tongue and ever growing confidence with the opposite sex would negate the need to pay for his pleasures.

The last part of my father's nautical training before being drafted was to undertake his trade training as a 'Stoker' and to receive the trained, engine room rating of 'Stoker 2nd Class'. On the face of it shovelling coal into a boiler does not seem the sort of job that required deep, meaningful training. But that would be to denigrate the trade and undervalue the man. There was much to learn. There were pressure gauges to observe, valves to turn on and off and pipework to be held in balanced pressure and to be repaired as required. In later life Emanuel would list one of his skills as 'pipe fitting'. He would have learned this specialist skill as a Stoker. On a more basic level, he was obliged to learn the management of the ash and clinker and with his comrades, to shovel thousands of tons of coal. It would take a day and a night of virtually the whole crew shovelling to fill the bunkers of a cruiser. The method employed a lighter which would come alongside the ship. A grab would lift the coal from the lighter and dump it on deck. The stokers would be down in the bunkers receiving the coal, "trimming" as they called it, to level off and balance the distribution. Sometimes the coal would need to be broken up which raised alarming levels of dust.

Much of the training would necessarily include the practical application of his newly acquired skills on board varying classes of ship. This would give Emanuel the experience required to handle the variety of steam boilers then in use by the Royal Navy. There was much to learn and memorize. A capital ship could have as many as thirty or forty coal fired boilers that would need to work in unison. Depending on the maintenance and the repair schedule complimented by the modification programme, not all boilers would be in use at any one time. There was always a need for boiler repair. Perhaps one of the least liked jobs was that of cleaning the boilers. This was hot, detested work in comparative darkness which would leave those involved covered in perspiration and caked with coal-dust. As time progressed, it began to dawn on Emanuel that being part of the engineering staff, although absorbing and physically demanding, also meant that he spent most of his time deep in the bowels of the ship where the atmosphere was dark, hot and humid with no respite from the dust or ash. The seeds of discontent were being sewn.

On February 3rd, 1913, Emanuel graduated from training, gaining his rating of Stoker second class. He was granted one day's local leave which included travelling time to go to the Dockyard at Portsmouth where he was to join HMS New Zealand. The New Zealand was a brand new battle-cruiser built on the Clyde and launched eighteen months earlier in 1911. At the dockside in the crisp February, sunlight, Emanuel looked on with complete amazement as the ship's shadow dwarfed him and the dockside sheds. What a magnificent ship. He had seen nothing like it in seventeen years of life. It was beyond anything that he could imagine. HMS New Zealand measured 590 feet and to Emanuel's amazement had thirty-one, hungry, coal-burning boilers to power the first generation of what were called steam turbine engines. She was state-of-the-art for the time, armed with eight, twelve-inch guns and had a top speed of 26 knots. When he picked up his posting details from the Chief Petty Officer, Emanuel had been told how lucky he was to be drafted to this ship which was part of what Admiral Jackie Fisher described as 'The New Navy to face the Kaiser'. Once he had seen the ship he could not believe his luck; this was more than he had hoped for.

Emanuel formally arrived on board, so the ship's log reports, in the late evening of February 5th, 1913 at 9.30 pm. He was one of four stoker-ratings drafted from the Devonport Coaling Ship at Plymouth where he had been temporarily located, pending the final posting to the New Zealand. He was directed straight away to the Stokers' mess below decks where a senior hand allocated him a place to sling his hammock and stow his ditty box. There were 110 stokers on the ship and individual space was at a premium. Most of the stokers were seasoned sailors and Emanuel and his compatriots had joined the ship late. This was to prove a great pity as many of the seamen had already been working together for some time and had bonded into their watches. For the first time in his young life Emanuel had to find himself in this micro society of seasoned men where individual presence and sometimes humility was everything. As he stowed his hammock and later joined the mess table for scran (food), he listened intently to the gossip. From time to time he would have attempted to join in the conversation, simply to confirm his identity; perhaps too, because he wanted to be noticed. That's what he did at the workhouse and it succeeded. It was not easy for him and he may initially have experienced peer rejection from his mess mates, or may have been antagonised by a single person? Alternatively, he may have tried too hard? The records are not clear.

HMS New Zealand

Come what may, everybody was talking about the Royal Inspection. His Majesty the King Emperor, George V had finished his inspection of the ship hours earlier at 3.55 pm in company with his cousin, Prince George of Battenberg (grandson of Queen Victoria). Prince George was to remain on board as part of the ship's company. For several days the crew had been working all hours to prepare the ship for the Royal inspection. Emanuel's late arrival and lack of involvement in these activities may have been resented by some of his mess mates. The vagaries of micro life patterns inside the tight, unforgiving society of the stokers' mess are anything but easy to understand or even to relate to. Nevertheless, this was a prestigious ship of the line. The icing on the cake was that HMS New Zealand was bound for a nine-month world cruise. It would take Emanuel to all those pink coloured countries he had daydreamed about when looking at the waxed map on the Holsworthy, classroom wall. His dreams were becoming a reality. The ship was scheduled to travel fifty thousand miles calling at St Vincent, Ascension Island, St Helena, Capetown, Durban and Melbourne before going on to New Zealand, Suva, Honolulu, Vancouver, Panama, Callao, and Valparaiso, before passing the Strait of Magellan and then on to Montevideo, Rio De Janeiro, the West Indies and home via Halifax NS. What a fantastic journey of a life time for a young man.

On February 8th 1913, bedecked in bunting, with the Royal Marine Band playing on the quayside and crowds waving and cheering, the ship slipped her moorings and made her way down the Solent towards the English Channel and the open sea. Emanuel had been on board just two days and was still finding his feet. We can only imagine the excitement that he must have felt at embarking on this momentous voyage and the pride in being selected to be part of this impressive ship's crew. From this high point in his life and new career, straight out of training, what followed is difficult to explain. In an extremely short period of time, motivation turned to despair and then de-motivation of the most profound kind. This seventeen-year-old sailor was now to meet his nemesis. Ninety years later it is hard to piece together exactly what happened as some historical records remain closed, but to those who have undertaken military or naval service, there may be a ring of truth in the following hypothesis.

When my father arrived to serve on the New Zealand he had a positive, faultless record. The transition to naval discipline and barrack life from the workhouse would likely have been more of the same so I doubt that upset him. Something happened on HMS New Zealand which caused an irreversible change in his character and that was to have profound implications in his later life. My father had everything to look forward to with the prospect of a twelve-year career with promotion opportunities for a bright lad. And Emanuel was a bright and adept lad.

The only indication of what happened to him lies in his all too brief record of service précis. This précis indicates that between February 6th and November 30th 1913, my father spent extended periods in the cells as a result of punishments awarded by Captain Halsey, Captain of HMS New Zealand. One of the most extraordinary aspects is that he was awarded a custodial sentence for the first offence. The expectation of the time and the present day is that naval and military punishment is progressive. A first offence for a seaman, straight out of recruit training would normally be treated leniently with a mild punishment of restriction of privileges, or a fine. For the first offence recorded on his conduct sheet my father was awarded seven days in the brig (cells). This suggests that he was accused of a very serious infraction. Records indicate that all of the disciplinary sentences are associated with landfall which coincided with: New Zealand, Fiji and Honolulu.

The full extents of the infractions are not known and an exhaustive search of Admiralty records at Kew has so far drawn a blank. There can be no doubting the periods of punishment awarded by Captain Halsey. In order they were: seven days, fourteen days and seven days, all in the cells, on board ship. On the fourth occasion, Captain Halsey felt that his powers of punishment were insufficient for whatever crime my father had committed. When this happens, the next step is for the Captain to "remand" the case for Courts Martial. This happened whilst HMS New Zealand was in port at Esquimalt, Vancouver Island, Canada. My father was clearly found guilty and sentenced.

The worst military and naval crime is to disobey an order or to challenge authority, be it right or wrong. Emanuel was nobody's fool and from the results of his latter life, he was probably much brighter and more capable than many who had command over him. Given the severity of the punishments awarded to my father, I suspect that he fell foul of one of those transgressions, probably involving a senior rating or a Petty Officer. This type of problem normally revolves around a personality clash where, regardless of the rights and wrongs, the captain would always back the system. From Captain Halsey's point of view, in the interests of maintaining the ship's discipline, he would want to teach my father a lesson and drive home that point of discipline to a young seaman. Such a punishment would also be viewed by other crew members as a warning and example.

On reading all the available information, my opinion is that someone probably made life hell for a young, gauche Emanuel. In response and it must be said probably naively, Emanuel attempted to resist this and fight 'the system'. There is a tiny clue on his record where the word "impertinence" (insolence, impudence, disrespect?) is written. I believe that this suggests that he was trying to stand up for himself and speak back in the face of what might have been an injustice. In the narrow, confined society of the Stokers' Mess, right or wrong, my father would have stood alone without backing. It would be foolhardy to contest naval authority knowing full well that if you did attempt to speak out, to condemn a superior rating or Petty Officer, the local retribution could be extremely painful and miserable. At worst, below deck life could be a 'dog eat dog' existence.

Captain Halsey would not have been blind to what was going on; maybe that is why he remanded my father's charge to a Courts Martial. A further clue from the records is that having been sentenced to fourteen days in the cells he destroys his uniform in open defiance by burning it. This is a powerful, childish statement that he wants no more of naval life! He has lost all confidence in naval justice! In today's world we might acknowledge that as a cry for help. Finally, after being sentenced to a further seven days in the cells, he decides enough is enough and he somehow escapes from the cells on board, only to be recaptured. This immature, but desperate attempt to run away from authority led to the final hearing before Captain Halsey who now had no alternative but to remand the case for Courts Martial. As we now know, the Courts Martial found him guilty and he was sentenced to ninety days detention to be served locally in Victoria, British Columbia. As yet, the Courts Martial papers remain closed until 2012 when they will be reviewed.

Two things happened to Emanuel as a result of his Royal Navy experience which left an impression on him that would remain for the rest of his life. In the first instance he lost all confidence and trust in authority of any kind, be it military or civil. He would never trust in the law again. Secondly, he would have nothing but contempt, disdain and disregard for the integrity of a court, be it civil or military. In the years to come Emanuel would make frequent appearances in court and when he did, he would conduct his own defence and whatever punishment or fine was imposed by the Court, he would ignore it with vitriolic contempt. Moreover, to make his presence felt, he would fervently object to a member of the court on one ground or another, as if challenging the legitimacy of the Court. This reaction, owes its origin to those fateful Navy days. The further irony is that such a reaction should come from a seventeen year old formerly used to the highly disciplined life of the workhouse.

At this juncture in its world cruise, HMS New Zealand was in port in the purpose-built naval facility at Esquimalt opposite Vancouver, on the beautiful Island of Victoria, British Columbia. Much to the relief of Captain Halsey, by the time Emanuel was scheduled to be released from prison, HMS New Zealand would have long since sailed from Canadian waters en route to Mexico, Panama and Valparaiso. He was no longer Captain Halsey's problem; instead he was now the responsibility of Captain Caplain, Esquimalt's senior naval officer who, himself, had not long been in post. Once Emanuel had been released from prison, Captain Caplain's solution was to draft him to the Pacific Squadron based at Esquimalt. On hearing this decision, the realisation now came to Emanuel that he would not be going back to England for a very long time, but instead, was destined to spend up to three or four years at this Canadian backwater before home leave would be granted.

In 1865 Esquimalt had replaced Valparaiso in Chile as the headquarters of the Royal Navy's Pacific Squadron. New docks, hospitals and barracks had been built there and located only five miles from the picturesque town of Victoria. It was a comfortable posting, but lacked the buzz of Plymouth. The Pacific Squadron was not particularly large or, it has to be said, effective. There were no defined threats in the area at this time, although by late 1913, the German raider Leipzig was to be recognised lurking further south in Mexican waters. The Pacific Squadron comprised two minor, lightly armoured ships, the sloops HMS Algerine and Shearwater. Both were a mixture of sail and steam and spent a pleasurable life sailing the Pacific stations, or at least that was the scuttlebutt voiced to Emanuel when he left prison.

But the truth of the matter was something different. The Pacific Squadron at that time was a dead end posting dreaded by most seamen. At the time of Emanuel's release from prison, a Court of Enquiry was under way regarding Commander Brooker, the Captain of HMS Algerine. The enquiry related to the breakdown in relations between the Captain and his officers. The enquiry noted that Commander Brooker had become a solitary person failing to communicate with his fellow officers or to display the leadership qualities to motivate and inspire the crew. It showed. The Court of

Enquiry opened by Commander Henslowe described the ship as unhappy with several members of the crew having drink problems. Far from sailing the Pacific Ocean, HMS Algerine spent most of her time in port. The other sloop, HMS Shearwater fared little better. To make matters worse, pay and rations for members of the crew were often in short supply or late in delivery, with local chandlers failing to provide goods because of unpaid Admiralty bills.

This was the environment that Emanuel entered on leaving Prison in Victoria. Once more, Stoker Second Class Mitchell was to feel deeply let down and de-motivated, this time by his posting to a dead-end ship, with a dead end Captain and a drunken crew. What he had not appreciated was that Algerine's new Captain, Commander Corbett, who was to join the ship on January 2nd 1914, was a very different kettle of fish from his predecessor with outstanding leadership skills, much liked and respected by his contemporaries.

HMS Algerine

On 11th October 1913, Algerine's ship's log records receiving one rating from, Detention Quarters (Late HMS New Zealand). That was my father. It also seems that he did not serve the full term of ninety days, instead earning remission after seventy-five days. Between

October 19th, 1913 and April 13th, 1914 my father served on one or other vessel for various cruises from Alaska in the north to Mexico and further south. In early April 1914, HMS Algerine was at anchor in the bay at San Diego, in the United States waiting for lighters to bring out coal from the USN Coaling Depot. Life had not taken an upward turn for my father, despite the fact that he improved his rating to Stoker 1st Class and received a character and ability rating of 'very good' from Captain Corbett. What he had achieved, however, was an ability to play the system just as he did at the workhouse. He was now biding his time before deciding what to do next.

On April 12th, 1914 HMS Algerine lay at anchor off San Diego, having the day before taken on its complement of coal and fresh supplies. As Emanuel lay in his hammock, he listened as the ship gently rocked on the tide. From time to time the noise of creaking ropes punctuated the air as the mast heads dipped and then arose with the swell, tensioning the rigging and then allowing it relax again. His eyes were wide open with his hands under his head. He was deep in thought as he gazed at the bright moonlight which streaked through the porthole casting razor sharp shadows on the white bulkhead of the Stokers' Mess. As he lay there, he felt the soft balmy, Pacific breeze across his exposed body. He had reached a momentous decision. He realised that the Royal Navy was no longer for him. 'They could go to hell.' Moreover, there was nothing to go back to Holsworthy for. His brothers and sisters had long dispersed to do the usual humdrum jobs associated for people of their station. Emanuel had no intention of doing the same. His year on a farm shovelling dung and every shitty job going had taught him that there must be more to life than that. But instead, he had traded shovelling dung for coal, and a life in grime and sweat in the confined, dark holds of a ship. This was not progress. This was a life in Hades. On the other hand, the United States was the New World. It was a place of hope and expectation and they did not give a tinker's cuss about the British, its class system or its Empire. Emanuel had made up his mind.

On his next run ashore, he was careful to secrete a few odds and ends in his ditty box, roll them up in some paper and carry them ashore, so he said, to get it repaired, whatever it was?

HMS Shearwater

Just when matters seemed to be personally improving and no one was watching him, Emanuel made the conscious decision to go absent without leave (AWOL). Although it is unlikely that he appreciated the fact at the time, he would have to live with this decision for the rest of his life haunted by the threat of the knock on the door, a shadow following him, or a hand on his shoulder that would lead to his arrest and return to prison. From now on, he would be a hunted man for desertion from the King's Navy. But somehow, that did not seem to matter.

Crew of HMS Shearwater Circa 1912

He now recalled all those tales that he had heard in Holsworthy as a boy about the opportunities in the United States of America and Canada. This was a big country and he could quickly lose himself, he thought. In any case, the Algerine would be gone on the morning tide. Tomorrow is another day, he thought, and the first day of my new life.

San Diego Circa 1913

Notes:

The railway line between Holsworthy and Exeter was closed during the 1960's as was the picturesque line across the edge of Dartmoor. HMS Vivid was re-named HMS Drake in 1934 and is still a main training base for RN ratings, although much of the dockyard has been sold off for superior housing. Aggie Weston's was re-built in the 1950's and is still providing sailors comforts ashore. Union Street is a shadow of its former self and has been largely redeveloped, although it is still a favoured haunt for sailors. The Palace Theatre is still there, but looking a bit shabby. HMS New Zealand enjoyed a wonderful world cruise and returned to England to take part in the Sea battles of WW1 becoming the Flagship for Admiral Beatty. She was decommissioned in 1922 and broken-up in 1923. Captain Halsey later became Admiral Sir Lionel Halsey in 1920. HMS Algerine and Shearwater were transferred to the Royal Canadian Navy and patrolled the Pacific until being sold in the 1920's. Esquimalt remains a key RCN base for the Pacific theatre. As to what a Dous might be is open to conjecture. Perhaps it is a corruption of the old Devonshire name of Dawe in this case meaning Dawes land.

Chapter 4

A New Start in the New World

On the morning of 14th April, 1914, Emanuel came down to the San Diego shoreline north of the US Navy Coaling station. As waves gently rolled and tumbled on to the beach in front of him, he watched HMS Algerine slip her anchor and head off out to sea. Emanuel remembered that sailing around North Island and into the Pacific was a difficult course to navigate. The telegraph in the engine room would often clang as the Captain called for varying speeds to safely navigate a route past the shallows, making sure the boat did not ground on the sand bars whipped up by the fast, Pacific current. He allowed himself one quick smile of contentment, but then quickly came to his senses. Those days were now over.

There is no doubt that at this time his mind was confused. He had made some good friends in the Pacific Squadron and the social life in Victoria, not far from Esquimalt, wasn't that bad. He also had to admit to himself that life on the Algerine and Shearwater had been pleasant enough, except for the drunkenness. However, now that Commander Brooker had departed and Commander Corbett had taken over, the general atmosphere on board had greatly improved and at least the officers had stopped bickering among themselves. But then his mood changed. He could not forgive or forget what happened to him on the New Zealand. After talking to a few crusty old salts, he also knew with a profound realisation that his naval career was over. It would be a long time before their Lordships at the Admiralty would forgive and forget his misdemeanours. In any case, Emanuel mused to himself, it was a totally undeserved blot that would stay for the remainder of his twelve-year contract with the Royal Navy. No, there was no future in the Navy.

At HMS Vivid and even up to the day he stood on the quayside at Portsmouth in the shadow of the New Zealand, he had high, idealistic thoughts of a great career in the Royal Navy. He had dreamt of finishing his career as the Master at Arms on a capital ship with a pension to follow. In comparison with his contemporary stokers, he knew that he was brighter and quicker than they were. These facets in his character had been noted during training and he knew that he had been singled out for the crew of the prestigious HMS New Zealand. He shook his head in disbelief at his present circumstances and momentarily felt exceptionally sorry for himself. He squeezed his hands until his knuckles were white, took a deep breath and looked once more at the receding HMS Algerine.

The afternoon before, soon after the liberty boat had discharged him on 'a run ashore' he had bought a pair of workman's trousers and a heavy cotton twill shirt from the sailors store down by the jetty, overlooking Coranado. Coranado was a delightful spot, popular with sailors and comprised the small settlement on North Island. Emanuel had heard that this was a good, cheap, shop and that their clothes were hardwearing. Over a drink in one of the local bars a week or so before he had met some US Marines garrisoned in Balboa Park and pumped them for all his worth for local information including, a cheap place for the night. He had confided in them his intention to go AWOL and being Americans, of course, there was every encouragement for him to do so and 'why not join the US Marine Corps?' He accepted their advice on cheap accommodation, but was reticent about exchanging one naval regime for another. Nevertheless, the billet recommended by the US Marines was adequate and inexpensive, albeit the cockroaches roaming this garret kept him awake with their clattering feet across the rough tiled floor. But that was not all; his mind was spinning as he anticipated his future. Had bravado given way to rank stupidity? It would be a certain jail sentence if he were caught. That night he tossed and turned as the devils and picklocks of indecision tormented his mind. The blanket under which he slept became sodden with sweat as the night progressed. When dawn came he was glad, but noticed that his right hand was trembling.

In the warm, dry atmosphere of a San Diego spring morning, he arose from his bed intent on seeing through his plans for a new life. Although, truth to tell, he was full of big ideas, actually, he had no idea beyond a general plan of what to do next. There was no detail to this seventeen-year-old's thought. He was very much a 'make it up as you go along' sort of man already displaying a tendency to make snap, ill thought-out decisions. His trembling ceased as his brain came to terms with his predicament. He methodically washed and dressed as if still in the navy, but now in the blue cotton twill shirt and trousers that he had bought the day before. He had kept the brown paper and string that the new clothes were wrapped-up in and re-used them to parcel-up the parts of his Royal Navy uniform that he no longer required. He had considered burning them, but quickly recalled that last time he had done that, he came a cropper! But how foolish to think that way, he wasn't in the Navy now. As he secured the parcel with string, he was once more transported back to HMS Vivid and the seemingly endless lessons on nautical knots. These were given by a particular Petty Officer who had a voice impediment, a lisp. 'This is a weef knot' the Petty Officer would say much to the amusement of the class. Now Emanuel smiled to himself before he took the parcel in his hands, paused and looked out to sea. Algerine looked serene and beautiful as she appeared to glide through the waves, rising and falling as she caught the white caps. She was now almost out of sight as she turned west to circumnavigate North Island for the open sea. Emanuel took a deep breath and sighed; then, with a heave and a grunt, he cast his bundle of naval clothes into the ocean. For a moment he watched as the current caught the package and took it out to sea. He then turned inland towards the town of San Diego to set off on the next part of his life.

Climatically, San Diego has to be one of the most pleasant spots in the United States. On this April morning, blossom was on the trees and the streets were teaming with people beautifully tanned by the ever present sun, eager to go about their business. And there was most certainly plenty of that. San Diego was a thriving, prosperous town. Emanuel had already worked out that he could obtain plenty of casual work either on one of the many farms and ranches, or in town with one of the merchants or tradesmen. After all, he knew the basics of plumbing and could join pipes together and had some farm experience. History also interested him and in speaking to locals over the bar he soon became aware that San Diego was originally a Spanish colony later incorporated into Mexico. The United States had gained sovereignty following the Mexican-American war of 1846, he was advised. When the Santa Fe Railroad arrived in 1884, the population simply multiplied. Emanuel felt enlivened and buoyant at the prospects that he heard. This was so different from Holsworthy or Plymouth.

The connection between San Diego and the Royal Navy was simple; coal. Opposite Coronado was the United States Navy Coaling station. It had been a significant U.S. coaling station since 1907 and in the early days provided much needed employment and income to the town. Along with the Navy came the Marines as Emanuel well knew. Not far away at Balboa Park was the small United States Marine Corps garrison. Just two days before, on April 12th during a run ashore, Emanuel had witnessed all the local excitement. Word was that 'big-wigs' were coming from Washington, including someone called FD Roosevelt, to open the Cabrillo Bridge. There was great excitement about this bridge which spanned a gorge, hitherto uncrossable. In its own right it was a civil engineering masterpiece, but most of all, it would give road access to the planned site for the Panama-California exposition of 1915. San Diego was coming of age. The festivities of the moment were still evident when Emanuel left the sea shore to set off for downtown San Diego. He naturally avoided the naval base and headed up towards Grant Hill. There he found shade under a tree, sat down and pondered a while. What to do next? He decided that the best thing was to go back to East Harbor Road and ask around in the bars if they knew of work opportunities. For the time being, he thought, it would be better to find work out of town, away from any possible shore patrol.

Constructing the Cabrillo Bridge 1913

Emanuel was neither as clever nor as resourceful as his circumstances now demanded. He was, after all, only seventeen years of age. The qualities of determination, resolution and self sufficiency seemed to be wafer thin in his personality. He was essentially an institutionalised boy where the day to day needs for his survival were provided on tap, first by the workhouse and then by the Royal Navy. Once that umbilical chord had been taken away and he had to rely on his own judgement he began "punching at life far above his weight," destined to meet disaster head on. Furthermore, his judgement was deeply flawed. There are people in life who have grandiose ideas, and very talented people who not only have an idea, but can make it work, sometimes to great profitability. My father was regrettably of the former type, at least in his formative years. But he would learn. Between April and November 1914 he walked the streets of San Diego achieving precious little. There being no workhouse or similar institution in the United States he was at first bereft of ideas on where to go when the going got tough. He had probably been told by the flotsam of San Diego street life that if all else failed, being arrested would get him a bed and square meals for a few days. One can imagine Emanuel's ears pricking up at this. Prison or jail for Emanuel held no horrors. He was no stranger to a few days in "stir" and in fact, may have looked forward to it. Intentionally or not, (I rather think intentionally) my father set the bait by being a nuisance and was duly arrested. On November 21st, 1914, the local sheriff cuffed him for vagrancy and the jail door once more closed on him for a fifth time. He was just four months over eighteen years of age.

Being arrested was one thing, but my father was clearly concerned about his desertion from the Royal Navy, should the Sheriff find out. The simple solution, so he argued to himself, was for him to become someone else. So he did. He gave the Sheriff the false surname of Childs, but using his real Christian names, claiming (which was true) to come from Devon, England. The irony here is that the American authorities were not in the least bit interested in my father's desertion from the Royal Navy. There was certainly no extradition treaty between our two nations and England was the old colonial power from whom America would accept no truck. In due course, father's case came up before the local Justice. He was sentenced to 180 days in the Sheriff's custody. Given the severity of his sentence, he must have made quite a nuisance of himself prior to arrest. Nevertheless, he was back in an institution and someone else was looking after him. He was content for the moment.

By early January 1915, far less than the 180 days' detention he was awarded, Emanuel was once more on the streets of San Diego; but not for long. In the same month, he was again arrested and appeared before the Justice Court in San Diego for forgery of "several" cheques. Luckily for him, on this occasion, the case was dismissed for lack of evidence. But he had stumbled across the trickster's favourite tool, the cheque book fraud. The theory being that, as long as there were cheques to write, there was money or goods to be had. Moreover, you could always sell again what you had bought with a forged cheque.

Between January and November 1915, with no inclination to find regular work and still clearly living off forged cheques, my father was once more roaming the streets of San Diego. His now near fluent silver tongue, complimented by a cheerful personality, had convinced others of his probity. He looked and sounded the part of a handsome, young gentleman The gullible, it would seem, readily parted with money or goods at his presentation of a simple slip of useless paper providing a fake promise. In the autumn of 1915, thanks to an infection, I suspect a touch of TB, Emanuel needed medical attention. He consulted a local Doctor named Learn. In payment for his services, my father passed over a cheque made out to a Mr Edward Carson for $10.50 which the doctor was asked to cash in order to extract his fee and no doubt give my father the change. He did and it bounced! Dr Learn reported the matter to the Sheriff. A warrant for my father's arrest was issued on February 17th, 1916. On March 6th 1916, the Superior Court of the County of San Diego heard the case and the presiding Judge, The Hon T L Lewis, sentenced my father, (now called Emanuel Frederick Mitchell Childs) to one year in San Quentin prison.

One of the telling documents of this time is the probation report commissioned by Judge Lewis prior to sentencing. This report gives insight into my father's mental condition at the time. In this report, Mr Blair, the probation officer, presented a summary of available information provided by my father. It makes bizarre reading. My father claimed to Mr Blair that he was 'the son of an Austrian Attorney'. He further claimed to be in the service of the English Government prosecuting minor cases on behalf of the Captain of HMS Shearwater. His story was that he had been sent to Victoria, British Columbia, on December 5th 1912. He went on to say that he had been advised by his physician to remain in the United States for health reasons! There may have been a grain of truth in this. A separate medical report also commissioned by Judge Lewis states that my father had "haemorrhage of the lungs". As if to shock the examining doctor my father added that he was mentally unbalanced and that it would be unsafe to grant him probation. Mr Blair took this as an indication that for one reason or another my father had probably upset the low life of San Diego and wanted to be locked away, out of harm's way. Mr Spencer, the District Attorney (DA), agreed that probation was not a good idea and suggested that my father needed medical help as he was 'addicted to the habit of forgery'! The District Attorney also suspected, so he noted, that my father had deserted from HMS Shearwater, but he did not recommend any further action to contact the English authorities.

One interpretation of what happened in San Diego is that after deserting the Royal Navy, work was harder to find than my father had previously thought. Another is that he had reverted to type? It is worth remembering that his mentors in the workhouse and in the Stokers Mess of the Royal Navy were all drawn from the lower ranks of society. When he found himself penniless and cornered, his survival instinct brought back into mind stories he had been told of scams and ruses to obtain cash. For the intelligent, articulate criminal with presence, and Emanuel was certainly that, fraud through confidence trickery was the ideal tool to lever open the wallets of the susceptible.

My father served the full term in jail inclusive of the two months in custody and ten months in San Quentin Prison. He was released on January 10th 1917. How sobering an experience prison was may be seen in what happened during the rest of his life where he showed no fear or apparent emotion at re-entering prison, confrontation with the law or standing up for himself. For the institutionalised boy, prison was, simply, another sanctuary; a sanctuary that enhanced his criminal knowledge. San Quentin prison housed some of the worst and cleverest criminals ever to be seen in the United States. There is little doubt that he would have spent time through natural gravitation with the more articulate white collar crooks. I suspect that it was here that he learned of the benefit of using aliases to hinder detection by the authorities. He would have been told how difficult it was in America to trace felons across the many states. "Use a different name and it will take forever to find you," he was advised. Not all of the instances of my father's indiscretions have been independently filed against name and criminal charge. But a list had been compiled with his assistance of some of the names he used. These included: James E Smith, LL Moody, Edward Mitchell, OP Johnson, Charles B Collins, and George Thomas, to name just a few. In later testimony, my father only ever owned up to using the surnames Thomas and Childs. To own up to others may have admitted liability for other misdoings for which the penalty may have been more severe. It does seem however that on his release from San Quentin in 1916, the seed of the serial fraudster had been sown, although it would lie dormant for a while. The relevance of the name Thomas will appear later. He never used the name Childs again.

St Quentin Prison, 1910

Perhaps it was a chance encounter, or a form of rehabilitation directed from prison, but the next recorded information about Emanuel finds him working as a 'ranch labourer'. His employer was a Mr McClain who lived 'fifty miles from San Diego'; hardly a specific address, but the sort of incomplete information that Emanuel was always to supply when questioned by the authorities. Judging by the name, Mr McClain was Scottish by ancestry. This proved to be a most profitable and opportune encounter. Having reached rock bottom in his life complete with a prison record, he was now about to re-invent himself with a plausible past. He listened intently to what the McLain family told him of their past in Scotland, where they had lived and what they did. What he learned provided the cloaking for his new persona.

Prison Record of my Father, St Quentin, 1916

When he next completed a government form, a new Emanuel Frederick Mitchell emerges, but now born in 1892. He then goes on confidently to write in bold, copper-plate handwriting that he is Scottish, born at Leith, close to Edinburgh and was previously a pipe fitter. To add that bit of gloss, he is pleased to inform that he was also a private soldier in the Seaforth Highlanders, Territorial Army (National Guard equivalent) from 1911 to 13. Of course, it was all baloney. There is little doubt that he gained all the Scottish information from the McClain family who may have been first generation immigrants to the USA. There is no record of my father ever visiting Scotland. Nevertheless, it was a clever ploy and he used this disguise successfully for several years, even to the extent that his children in America and their children continued to believe he was of Scottish ancestry. Inevitably, the authorities would find him out at a later and more sensitive time, but never completely.

During the time that my father worked for Mr McClain, the talk at home and locally was about the war in Europe, although the US was yet to enter the fray. For some time President Woodrow Wilson had maintained a strict policy of non-involvement. The sinking of the Lusitania in May, 1915 and further U boat attacks against US shipping was considered regrettable, but certainly insufficient for President

Wilson to go to war. 'This was essentially a European war' so the politicians on Capitol Hill advised. They wanted no part of it. However, on March 1st 1917, President Wilson exposed the infamous Zimmerman Telegram to the American public. This telegram, sent between Germany and Mexico, had been intercepted by the British Secret Service and was in the hands of Winston Churchill. On Prime Minister Lloyd George's instructions it was handed to Walter Page, the American ambassador in England, who dutifully passed it to President Wilson. The contents were shattering; if Mexico were to declare war against America, Germany would ensure that a great deal of the South West United States was handed back to Mexican sovereignty, once the war was won. This, so President Wilson exclaimed, was intolerable interference in the affairs of the United States. On April 2nd President Wilson asked congress for a declaration of war against Germany. As history now records, the United States declared war against Germany on April 6th 1917.

Almost immediately the US Army and National Guard began a recruiting campaign in preparation for mobilisation. Posters adorned buildings everywhere with Uncle Sam in his now customary top hat inviting the youth of America to answer the call to duty. A little over a month after the declaration of war, my father answered that call. He saw this as his chance to support his adopted country, without declaring his previous desertion from the Royal Navy. Perhaps this would redeem him somewhat? He would always be troubled that his desertion from the Royal Navy in 1914, if it were ever made public, might be confused with cowardice. In May 1917, he made his way to the headquarters of the National Guard, Division No 2, based in the San Diego-Federal Building, California. Here, he duly registered and signed-on for service in the US Army on May 24th. His enlistment papers described him as being a 'ranch-hand of Scottish ancestry and a former soldier in the Seaforth Highlanders. (No surprises there). He had by then clearly left the employment of Mr McClain for he now stated that he was living in the Golden Chest Hotel, San Diego. Presumably, he soon expected to be called forward and only anticipated a brief stay of a few days. As laudable as Emanuel's offer was, regrettably the US Army was not ready for him, or the many other recruits who had initially rallied to the Colours. The expansion of the US Army would take time to organise and Emanuel must wait patiently. In the meantime, he had to feed and accommodate himself. That required money of which Emanuel had very little saved from his four months work on Mr McClain's ranch.

If nothing else in his life, my father was resourceful and would attempt to turn his hand to anything that might earn him a 'buck or two'. The trouble was that the 'anything' had incredibly flexible boundaries where matters of the law were concerned. It is very easy to be judgemental eighty years later, but survival may drive a man off the straight and narrow. The picture that always comes back is one of a scared man on the run, always looking over his shoulder, now with aliases and a prison record. This was not the ideal C.V. or résumé to put before an employer! More to the point, beyond his wit he had no identifiable skills that anyone might pay for, other than manual labour. Whilst he said that he was a 'pipe fitter' he never seemed to have pursued that trade. In May 1917, circumstances demanded that he needed to get a casual job that paid cash, preferably by the day.

North of San Diego, conveniently on the railway was the up and coming town of Los Angeles and close by in the suburbs, a place called Silver Lake. Here, and around the area which became known as Hollywood, several companies had set up to turn out the entertainment marvel of the time; moving pictures. From time to time Emanuel had visited moving picture theatres, or nickelodeons as they were called and thrilled at the adventures of a host of silent film stars. He particularly liked D W Griffith epics and Douglas Fairbanks and, of course, that English fellow with the funny walk, Charlie Chaplin. A new word had entered the national vocabulary which Emanuel would later use with an increasing frequency. A night at the film theatre would be 'going out to the flicks' which referred to the flickering light that illuminated those early films.

It was well known in the bars of Los Angeles and San Diego that there was money to be earned as a film extra. What's more, the money was paid in cash, often on a daily basis. A wink was as good as a nod to Emanuel. He had found the solution to his problems, whilst he waited to be called-up. He would take casual work as a film extra. All he had to do was board a train for Los Angeles and make his way to Silver Lakes, which was conveniently at the end of the line. He had heard that the Mack Sennett studios were always hiring extras for their comedy films. There were also a lot of English actors and extras there, particularly one called Stan Laurel who was beginning to make a name for himself. Whoever gave my father this lead, it proved to be a good one. In late May 1917 Emanuel invested what sums he had left in a train ticket, or perhaps he just hitched a ride on a railcar, and set off for the bright lights of Los Angeles. There he began work, as he later described it on government forms, as a 'moving picture actor'.

Mack Sennett Studios 1916

In subsequent years my father would talk casually to others about his life and experiences in Hollywood, name dropping about Mary Pickford, Gloria Swanson, Pola Negri, Stan Laurel, Douglas Fairbanks, Wallace Beery, Charlie Chaplin and Fatty Arbuckle to name but a few. Everyone, of course, thought it total bullshit, or at best a flight of fancy. But like much else that he came out with, there was always a grain of truth in the story. He knew them all, he said, and he had appeared in some films in which they starred. He never tried to suggest that he was anything more than an extra, a bit player, or that his relationship was anything more than as an acquaintance, but he did say that the work was fun and he made a lot of friends with whom he kept contact after the war. That part was at least true as his children recalled being "baby sat" by the stars. Hearsay has it that it was post WW1 that amorous letters passed between my father and the silent film star Mary Pickford; letters found and kept by Irene. At the time, Miss Pickford was enjoying a relationship with Howard Hughes. As with so much about my father, there is always a strand of truth in what is recounted. The question arises, was this liaison the cause of a stab wound father later recounted to my sister, Thelma? Had he received a visitation from Mr Hughes' associates? Certainly Howard Hughes was not a man to cross and the date coincides with the ending of my father's Hollywood aspirations in 1920, but more sadly the beginning of his infidelity to Irene.

The staple of the Mack Sennett studios was knock about comedies like the frenetic episodes involving the Key Stone Cops. The reader may remember that the policemen wore a rather large star on their uniforms. This is significant. Please keep that in mind for later. Whatever Emanuel did, he was paid about $3 a day with food thrown in at the studio canteen. All he had to do was to find a cheap lodging house which he described on another government form as the 'Hotel Fortune, Los Angeles'; an apt name in his case. These were times of milk and honey and money up front. But most of all, he enjoyed considerable personal happiness and perhaps even success. As early photographs reveal, he was good looking in a youthful, boyish way and may have photographed well. But, as in all Hollywood stories, the good times have to give way to reality.

On September 20th, 1917, just as the first winds of autumn were being felt and the requirement for film extras was diminishing, my father visited the Canadian Consulate in Los Angeles. He may have been tired of waiting for the US Army to call him, or having spoken with other British expatriates at Silver City, decided to do something there and then for King and Country. In late 1917 the war was not going well for the British. The Germans had announced unrestricted submarine warfare and on land the battles at Messines, Passchendaele and the Somme had ravaged the British and Canadian armies. The war assessment was bleak. How much this affected Emanuel is open to conjecture, but four months after signing on for the US Army and after a brief acting career in films, he decided to enlist in the Canadian Army and did so on September 20th, 1917. The consulate provided him with travel documents and once more he was bound for Victoria, Vancouver Island, BC, to join the 1st depot Battalion, British Columbia Regiment ((Duke of Connaught's Own) based in Vancouver. On enlistment, he gave an incorrect date of birth (1891) but continued the cover story of being Scottish, born in Edinburgh, a pipe fitter by trade and having had service with the Seaforth Highlanders! Well, it worked the last time, why not? He further identified his father and next of kin as Mr John Mitchell, who was now to be found, care of his sister Mary, with the address of City of London Mental Hospital, England. Somehow, despite his adventurous life, Emanuel had remained in contact with his sister Mary.

In early October 1917, less than three years after arriving on Vancouver Island with the Royal Navy, Emanuel returned in a different guise. If he felt vulnerable or tense at the possibility of his Royal Navy desertion being discovered, the army did not pick up the vibrations. He completed the various medical and administrative requirements at the mobilization centre in Victoria, before proceeding to Vancouver to be kitted out in government livery, but this time khaki! He was glad to be back in uniform where, as previously at the Holsworthy workhouse, living-in on the farm, serving with the navy at HMS Vivid and dare I say, in prison at San Quentin, he would be fed, clothed and looked after in the arms of a big institutional family. The bonus, or icing on his cake, was that he was back on a pay roll.

Emanuel officially enlisted in the Canadian Army on October 23rd 1917. He signed a contract at the mobilization centre in Victoria for one year's service plus six months at the end of hostilities or, for the duration of the war; how so ever long that was. He was then immediately posted to 1st Depot Battalion, British Columbia Regiment, Canadian Expeditionary Force. The drafting board had clearly taken into consideration his previous (fake) service in the Seaforth Highlanders, and waived basic training before sending him on his way. By now WW1 had been underway for three years and the recruiting machinery was well oiled and effective. Overall, the Dominion of Canada provided an army of five hundred and ninety five thousand men organised into two hundred and sixty numbered battalions. Of that number, some thirty-six thousand men were to give their lives for an island six thousand miles away. The Canadian Army distinguished itself at the various battles of Ypres, Vimy Ridge, Amiens and Arras, all close to or inside the Belgian border. In 1915, so Emanuel was advised in training, history recorded the first offensive use of gas warfare on totally undefended or prepared Canadian soldiers. By 1917, the use of chemical weapon bombardment using chlorine, phosgene and mustard gas was commonplace.

Canadian Regimental Aid Post Arras 1917

As Emanuel was soon to discover, the grizzly results of war are casualties. Taken as a whole during WW1, the Canadian Army was to suffer approximately one hundred and fifty-six thousand wounded. The administrative and logistic organisation necessary to manage the growing casualty lists of 1917–18 was also extensive. So much so, that an organisation had to be in place to repatriate the wounded back to Canada and from there to the required home province. My father was to join this organisation.

The Canadian Garrison Regiment was a hybrid organisation grown out of the need for exemplary administration and organisation across the Canadian provinces, to support the fighting units. The greater part of their work was to do with embarking and disembarking Canadian forces and supplies heading for the UK and then onward to France. Conversely, with an almost inexhaustible supply of returning wounded, there was a dire need for a dedicated organisation for casualty evacuation. The evacuation route followed a line from the aid posts operated in the trenches to the field ambulances behind the lines. From there the wounded were passed on to the field hospitals in France. Depending on the severity of the wound, casualties might then be passed to Army Hospitals in England and thence by rail and steamship for repatriation and final recovery back to Canada. For the most part, this work was under the auspices of the Canadian Army Medical Corps.

In Canada, the repatriation began at Camp Hill Hospital, Nova Scotia, where the wounded were taken from the quayside at Halifax. From there, dedicated hospital trains took them across Canada. The final destination, or the end of that recovery line, was the Thomas Shaughnessy Military Hospital, Vancouver.

It was to Camp Hill Hospital, that my father found himself posted in early December 1917. He had not been there very long when the perils of warfare were brought home to him in graphic, never to be forgotten detail. On December 6th 1917, early in the morning, the staff at Camp Hill Hospital witnessed a deafening explosion. Shock waves were felt all over Halifax and far beyond. The damage included the destruction of almost two square miles of housing in northern Halifax, totally flattened by the blast. Fires broke out everywhere. The death toll amounted to a staggering two thousand people, many of whom were civilian. History was to record this explosion as the biggest of WW1 and to the present day the biggest originating from conventional explosives. The cause had been the arrival of the French merchant ship, SS Mont Blanc, in-bound from New York with a highly unstable cargo of picric acid and TNT. Despite every precaution being taken to load and secure the cargo safely, on entry to the inner harbour at Halifax, the ship collided with the quay. That was enough to detonate the cargo.

The Mont Blanc Disaster Halifax NS

On December 27th 1917, after helping with clear up operations following the Mont Blanc explosion my father reported sick with knee problems. He said that he had damaged his knee in 1911 playing football in San Francisco which was obviously a fabrication. In 1911 he was working on the Devon farm having left the workhouse the year before. The result, he said, was that he broke his knee cap which had to be 'wired' back together. The medical report was inconclusive, but downgraded my father from A2 to C1, a less physically robust assessment. Within days Emanuel returned to duty. For the remainder of the war he spent most of his time on medical escort duties between Halifax, Nova Scotia and Liverpool. He seems to have shown great promise in this work. It also stimulated a personal interest in medical matters. At the age of 21 years he was promoted to the rank of sergeant with extended responsibilities. Hospital ships were necessarily furnished with medical and operating facilities. From this time onward, Emanuel began an infatuation with medicine or more specifically, osteopathy. In some documents of the time, when asked for an occupation, he drops the 'moving picture actor' description, taking on the academic persona of 'student'. This indicates a firm change in his outlook and perhaps a late maturing. He was clearly motivated and inspired by what he saw and experienced and was befriended by doctors. He seemed particularly interested in the care and rehabilitation of casualties. During the long off duty hours on board ship, he began to study the available medical references and to observe the doctors at work. He also took time out to talk about the new science and treatment entitled 'osteopathy' – manipulative surgery.

Camp Hill Hospital Halifax 1917

If there is an upside to war, it is that progress is often accelerated in medical matters as new techniques, drugs and treatments are used to save lives. One of the big advances, for example, was the breakthrough in blood transfusions pioneered in Canada; another was in the rehabilitation of the wounded. For the first time, forms of manipulative surgery were being practised as essential treatments for those who had suffered limb and spinal injuries or just to relieve the pressure on trapped nerves. There had been some extremely beneficial results, although in 1918, the results were devoid of the accompanying academic papers that would be needed to support clinical results. On and off for the next five years my father took an increasing interest in osteopathy. He studied assiduously, working and describing himself as a doctor of osteopathy in later life. However, his enthusiasm for this new branch in medicine was not always shared by the 'orthodox' medical profession. On the contrary, in the 1920's and 30's the medical establishment regarded osteopathy as no better than quackery! Little did he know it, and with the best of intentions, Emanuel was once more on the road to conflict.

But all this lay in the future, for the time being, my father was extremely happy in his work, either in port at Halifax or at Camp Hill Hospital, or crossing the Atlantic. After the terrible disaster of the Mont Blanc, the military medical machine had dove-tailed with the civilian medical establishment in Halifax to spread their resources, to recover from the dreadful carnage and destruction. When in port, Emanuel supported the combined effort. It was whilst liaising with the staff of Halifax Infirmary that early in 1918 my father first met an extremely attractive, if diminutive nurse called Irene Bailey.

****

Like Emanuel, Irene was born in 1896. Her home was in the Sydney township of Cape Breton Island on the north east tip of Nova Scotia. It was a wild and beautiful place. Irene was born into this progressive and bustling community to be the second of six daughters born to David and Jennie Thomas who were a second generation immigrant family from England. Of all the girls, Irene was said to be the most independent spirited, a trait greatly admired by Emanuel. Her deportment was the very model of Victorian-Edwardian society. At just 4ft 10 in stature, she was diminutive and devilishly attractive as Emanuel surmised from the corner of his eye.

He observed her for some time, before they were introduced. Emanuel had an eye for an attractive woman. He already enjoyed a vibrant sex life in down town Halifax to the extent that an early encounter with one of the, 'ladies of the night', so his medical record indicated, had led him to be treated for a sexual infection. This apart, his confidence with the ladies was legendary in barrack gossip, but he had no intention of settling down. Nevertheless, he was very taken by the pale, winsome complexion and dark curly hair that drew from her white, starched nurse's head dress and her trim, wasp-waisted body. He was now blatantly staring at her, absorbing every inch of her beauty still focusing on her red cross marked apron. She turned in his direction and he caught her highlighted profile against the background sun. He was again aroused by her figure; especially the well proportioned breasts that were clearly defined against her starched, white apron. Yet, at the same time, he noted a great sadness in her pale blue eyes. It was as though she had been crying for some time. There were dark shadows around her eyes which made them appear sunken and hollow. On the other hand, Emanuel was resplendent in his army uniform, his puttees patiently and evenly wound to ensure the best presentation. His black boots were gleaming and the three stripes on each khaki jacketed arm had been neatly whitened as if to exaggerate his importance. To finish this presentation of masculinity and perfection, the brass buckles of his webbing belt were burnished, glinting in the morning sun light. Nothing impressed officers more than a good turn out. Emanuel was not slow to catch on to this essential facet of military life. Just then, Irene caught Emanuel's eye. She wondered about the identity of the smart, good-looking young sergeant who was so openly staring at her.

It happened that Irene was just finishing her shift in the infirmary and was about to walk back to the nurses' hostel, down the hill away from the hospital, when my father, never slow with the ladies, introduced himself. They passed the time pleasantly talking about general matters, the war, the recovery from the disaster and of course the fall back of every Englishman, the weather. Emanuel found warmth in the conversation that reminded him of the better things in life. She was not only extremely attractive, he thought, but she spoke well and her conversation was engaging, interesting and educated. He wanted to see more of her. Before they parted company he was quick to make a later rendezvous. From then on they dated regularly whenever time allowed. The public gardens on the corner of South Park Street and Spring Garden Road, was a favourite meeting place. Here they could both escape the war. These were said to be the most beautiful Public Gardens in all of Canada. To Emanuel, it reminded him of happier Sunday afternoons in Victoria Park, Holsworthy. But these Halifax gardens were much more manicured and far more extensive with ducks on the pond! Irene liked the beautiful array of flowers that brightened up the dullness of some of those grey, wartime days. She found it consoling to sit by the fountains, shut her eyes and listen to the water playing around the statuary. It was so peaceful. As she shut her eyes she was drawn back to earlier times.

Victoria Park Bandstand 1915

On Sunday afternoons, before the war, she and Aaron would come to this Park where they would sit by the bandstand and listen to the Nova Scotia Regimental band playing military tunes or airs from the popular operettas. A brief smile broke over her face as she remembered that Aaron knew only two tunes, he said, one was the National Anthem, the other wasn't! After the concert they would walk hand in hand through the arboretum of specimen trees content in each other's company and young love. Emanuel caught the brief smile on her face as they sat by the fountain. Gazing into her closed eyes, he thought how pretty she was only to be caught as Irene opened her eyes. They looked at each other in the way that only lovers can. There were no words to explain what they really wanted to say to each other. It was all lost in the emotion of tragedy and deep affection. As they both pondered this moment Irene was the first to conclude that now was the right time to unburden her heart totally.

It was a tragic story, the kind of which Emanuel had heard several times before, which never failed to evoke deep sympathy within him.

After all, his beginnings were tragic enough. In 1915, so Irene described, she had married Aaron Bailey who was from Newfoundland and had secured labouring work in Halifax. At age eighteen in 1915, they had set up home together in a rented apartment in Halifax. Almost immediately after getting married, Aaron answered the call to duty and joined the Nova Scotia Regiment of the Canadian Infantry. He was four years older than Irene. After recruit training, he joined the Canadian Expeditionary Force and found himself 'in the line' not far from Ypres in Belgium. He was killed in action on April 27th, 1916 at the age of twenty two years.

Nobody thinks that they are going to die, even in war. It is always somebody else and this was very much the philosophy that Aaron and Irene adopted. But a double tragedy was to face Irene as she discovered, coincidently, that not only had Aaron been killed in action, but that she was also pregnant. She immediately fell into a deep, stunned malaise. It was never going to happen to her. Aaron was so strong. All of the plans that they had made together, all of her dreams were shattered. The depression that she now entered was deep, dark and unforgiving with a relentless ache in her heart. It was not surprising that she lost her baby through abject sadness and misery. There was now no remembrance of Aaron. She wept inconsolably. In time, help came from friends, family and the church and her wounded soul healed. She gathered her inner strength and resolve and realised that she must take up her responsibilities in life once more. There would now be many who would need her help and loving support to deal with their own bereavements from the Great War. As a nurse, she could now speak as one who knows. She returned to nursing.

Casualty ship that sailed between France-Southampton-Halifax.
(Sunk in 1917 with the loss of 123 lives)

Throughout 1918, the relationship with Emanuel flowered. Irene once more found a comfort and companionship that gradually blossomed into love. She liked the image that she saw of Emanuel in his crisp, neatly pressed uniform and peaked cap. He spoke well and confidently as a man who knew what he wanted and where he was going. He was to be a doctor after the war, he said, it was just a matter of time. He was learning everything he could with the Canadian Army Medical Corps doctors. When not talking to her about the future, Emanuel regaled her with stories of his early life in Hollywood and how he had met the stars. The future, he concluded was to return to America after the war, study osteopathy and set himself up in practice. This was the way ahead and this new medical practice offered a host of opportunities, he had told her. Irene was both supportive and excited by this worldly young man, although he was, in truth, the same age. He had done so much in his young life, seen so much and on top of everything, he was physically attractive to her and a wonderful lover. She was now both exhilarated and frightened that she might lose him. Once more, her heart ached. Sometime around Christmas or New Year 1918/19, Irene gave herself to Emanuel. Very soon it was clear that she was pregnant.

A little earlier, Emanuel and Irene had celebrated the armistice on November 11th 1918. It is probable that this was the date of conception. More to the point the armistice set Emanuel thinking about the future. In the next few months, hundreds of thousands of troops would be returning from the front and demanding demobilisation. Emanuel knew that as he had been employed away from the front, he would be among the last to be demobilised; perhaps it was six or nine months away or longer? He also knew exactly what he wanted to do in his future life. He felt an urgency and impetuousness to resume his civilian life that in any other circumstances might have been seen as laudable. To hasten matters along he was to play the Army system against itself to achieve early release; and by what better way than a medical discharge. He reported sick on December 10th 1918, Camp Hill Hospital, Halifax complaining once more of his left knee and how his work in casualty evacuation had aggravated an old injury. He was, as we would say today, playing the band! On January 24th, 1919, he was transferred by hospital train to Vancouver Military Hospital and on February 1st moved again to Thomas Shaughnessy Military Hospital, Vancouver. The upshot was that he was medically boarded and discharged from the Canadian army on March 20th, 1919.

Another example of my father's wacky form filling can be found in the information that he provided in March 1919 on the 'Medical History of an Invalid', prior to being boarded for discharge. He gave his home address as Arlington Hotel, Santa Barbara, California and resurrects his mother, Elizabeth (who died in 1898) as his next of kin and living at Imperial Valley California! He further gives his occupation as, 'Student' which seems to confirm that he wishes to continue with his studies to become an osteopath. Finally, he reiterates that the original date of the knee accident was 1911, playing football in San Francisco. This, of course, was totally untrue as at that time he was employed by farmer Druford at High Bickington (1911 census). When the injury actually took place remains a mystery. At that time Emanuel would have been 15 years old, a year out from the workhouse and presumably working on a local farm. No details have been found in the census. He may already have absconded from the farm that he was placed on, living the life of a vagrant. But it is possible to make an educated guess as to this injury. It would be unlikely that it happened on the farm as the injury would have been present at his Royal Navy medical when he applied to sign-on. Bearing in mind the high levels of physical activity required in stoking, I doubt that he would have passed muster with such an obvious injury. The more likely story (and where later there will be a sense of irony), is that it happened during his Royal Navy service where an operation would have been a little more feasible, and could have been done by a naval surgeon in the RN Hospital, Devonport. The resurrection of his mother, on the other hand, was no doubt a little piece of fraud to obtain travel documents at the government's expense, to go 'home'; home being America. It had not taken Emanuel long to learn how to play the Canadian army system!

Sometime around mid February 1919, Irene will have made Emanuel aware of her pregnancy. She was once more distraught with fear, this time realising how angry her parents and Aaron's family would be. For her it was a no win situation. Emanuel was not unsympathetic and indeed, probably felt real love and affection for her. In any case, he had wanted to include her in his long term plans; the announcement of her pregnancy only hastened matters. His proposition to her was to join him and move south to Los Angeles and to get married. She agreed. It would be better, in any case, that the marriage took place away from the prying eyes of her and Aaron's family. She meant no disrespect to her former husband's family, but it was just one more hurdle that, if it could be avoided, well, that would simplify matters.

During his terminal leave from the Army in March 1919, prior to his demobilisation, a now very confident and articulate Emanuel returned to Los Angeles by sea to pave the way for his bride-to-be and his future. He secured some accommodation in the Los Angeles suburbs with a promise of work near Oxnard. For the moment, money was not a problem. Emanuel was relatively rich with his final pay and gratuity and Irene had a few savings from her nursing work, but most of all she relied upon a small widow's pension from the Canadian government. In late March, Emanuel returned by boat to Vancouver plying that now very familiar route. On arrival in Victoria, he collected his demobilisation papers from the Regimental headquarters together with all outstanding pay and allowances. All that was now left was to await the arrival of Irene from Halifax on the Canadian Pacific railway, before setting off on the next stage in 'their' lives.

Notes:

The Royal Navy Pacific Squadron became the Royal Canadian Navy Squadron in 1916. The US Navy Coaling facility at San Diego became the home of the USN 6th Pacific fleet that later incorporated a huge naval air base on North Island. Similarly Camp Pendleton became a vast US Marine Corps training base and Marine Garrison. San Quentin Prison is still going strong. The British Columbia Regiment (Duke of Connaught's Own) based in Vancouver is now a reconnaissance regiment of the Canadian Army. The Canadian Army Medical Corps became the Royal Canadian Army Corps and is now the Medical Services Branch, Canadian Forces. The Camp Hill Veterans' Memorial Building (CHVMB) is located at the corner of Robie Street and Veterans Memorial Lane (the section of road between Robie and Summer Street). Shaughnessy Hospital Vancouver and the Red Cross Lodge have been rebuilt and offer extensive medical services including to veterans. The Gardens in Halifax remain as beautiful and enchanting as ever. When in later years the Mitchell family tried to research their Scottish ancestor, every search drew a blank which ensured that the myth lived on until 2006. For more on the Mont Blanc disaster, Halifax Museum website is excellent.

The descriptive paragraphs that weave together the story, although based on fact through accessible records, are for the most a product of imagination placing myself in my father's shoes and how I might have reacted. I will maintain this style throughout the remainder of the book. I am sure that it cannot be far from the truth.

Chapter 5

New Prospects Turn to Failure

In June 1919, with his demobilisation behind him and a wallet relatively full of cash, Irene and Emanuel made the sea journey from Vancouver to Los Angeles. From there, they travelled to the small town of Oxnard, about eighteen miles North West of Los Angeles. The name Oxnard was derived from its founder Henry Oxnard, the proprietor of the local American Beet Sugar (ABS) Company.

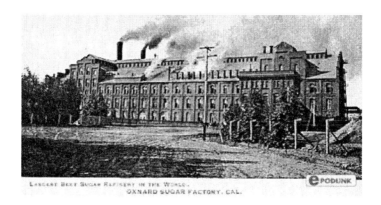

Oxnard Sugar Factory 1919

Emanuel was now brimming over with confidence and enthusiasm for his new career. For the moment, however, he was working for the ABS Company as a clerk. Irene was simply caught up in all the excitement and not unnaturally anxious to be settled for the birth of her first child. In the June 20th edition of the Oxnard Courier Irene and Emanuel's marriage announcement was reported. Emanuel was described as, 'a returning Canadian soldier' who was in the employ of the ABS Company and Irene, his intended, was from Nova

Scotia. During a visit to Oxnard in March, whilst on leave from Canada, my father had paved the way by securing the ABS job. At the same time, he made the acquaintance of Mr and Mrs J T Timberlake. So charmed were the Timberlake's by Emanuel's respectful personality and charm that they generously invited both him and Irene to stay with them pending their marriage. Mr Timberlake was a coffee storeowner. He was also a man of some standing in the community and would obviously be useful in fulfilling Emanuel's future ambitions. He also had a drug store and various other commercial interests.

The final part of the Oxnard wedding announcement, described how the happy couple would be, 'leaving for Peace Valley in Canada where they were going to homestead land provided by the Canadian government for returning veterans.' So far, nothing seemed to add up. More to the point, no land had been assigned by the Canadian Government to Sergeant Mitchell, or to Irene Bailey, as a result of her first husband's service. There was a small war service gratuity, some back pay and expenses, but nothing more. As for the job with ABS, it now seemed that it was little more than a stopgap. Irene had been unwittingly sucked into Emanuel's fantasy world and nefarious plans. At the time, I doubt that she thought twice about matters. Why should she? She was in love with Emanuel, they were to be married, and there was only a glorious future to look forward to starting in this beautiful, sunny part of California. On a darker side, I doubt that Irene had fully realised that on re-marriage she would forfeit the financial independence of her small, widow's pension paid by the Canadian Government.

Nevertheless, on June 16th 1919, Irene and Emanuel were married in Los Angeles. The ceremony was conducted by the Reverend William MacCormack, a distinguished cleric who later went on to become the Roman Catholic Bishop of New York. When after the ceremony Emanuel was required to complete the register, he deliberately falsified the records by declaring on the marriage licence that he was Scottish. This was most surely to guarantee that his cover remained intact. The authorities would not be looking for a Scottish Mr Mitchell who had been a naval deserter from San Diego. In fact, the authorities would not be looking for him at all. He continued the fiction by recording that his mother and father were also Scottish.

****

The social and cultural environment inside 1920 America was one of change, counter change and of a nation coming to terms with its broad ethnic mix. An American culture was struggling to be born tempered by a myriad of races, mostly European that had settled on the pacific seaboard. There had always been a feeling amongst many immigrants that America was, 'The Promised Land' and, therefore, its people owed a duty of devotion to God, in return for their deliverance. This somehow had become part of the national psyche and to a certain extent still is. There was also a feeling amongst many that God had prevailed and given the United States victory in the Great War. Emanuel by now, given what he had seen in the Great War, was a confirmed sceptic. Whilst he supported Irene in her faith, or at least did so on the surface, he had little time for pious churchmen. Nevertheless, he was perceptive enough to play the right role at the right time, when it was needed. He would now try to become a model American in this, religious, respectful society.

Amongst the nation as a whole there was enormous relief at the ending of the war with a wonderful feeling that the commercial growth, employment and prosperity, brought by the war, would extend into the next decade. And of course it did until the stock market collapse at the end of the second decade. The opportunities were there for Emanuel if only he could avail himself. Along with the religious fervour of the time came a perverse form of political correctness which would also colour the next two decades and impact on my father's life: prohibition. That is not to say my father was a drunk. On the contrary, he limited his drinking quite considerably and professed not to have much of a taste for alcohol. But that apart, drunkenness in the United States was considered and punished as 'an abuse in front of God.' American society saw the only way to stem this weakness was to prohibit it happening. In effect, the power of the established church was flexing its muscles through Congress to exercise control over society.

On January 16th, 1920, by means of the Eighteenth Amendment to the United States Constitution, Prohibition began. The prohibition regulations outlawed the manufacture, sale, importation and distribution of all alcoholic beverages. However, there was a loophole. Under the Eighteenth Amendment, as strange as that may now seem, the drinking and possession of alcohol were never made illegal in your own home. This was a fine subtlety which provided a grand opening for crime. Thus, overnight, the only access to alcoholic drinks came by smuggling from either Mexico or Canada. While some efforts were made in Canada to follow the United States example of prohibition, the general feeling there was not to impose such draconian laws. It is also worth remembering that Canada had a huge Scottish population that was very unlikely to vote against its own preferred beverage!

As one door closes another opens. Prohibition brought with it opportunities for crime. The cross border smuggling of alcohol is now part of the Great American Legend and has been brought to life in countless black and white movies, always it seems involving dumb blondes and machine guns. I think that the point to be made is that far from a gentle sport of cheating the customs official, this became a multi-billion dollar industry where human life was expendable. One of the finest aficionados of the time was Captain William McCoy who sprang to notoriety and introduced a quality standard for illicit alcoholic beverages in the expression, 'it's the real McCoy.' Bootlegging, as it was known, became a crime industry and offered easy money to those who dared, until the prohibition laws were repealed in 1933. My father became a passive observer of the halcyon days of dumb blondes, machine guns, illicit drinking, speakeasies, moonshine, and gangsterism. Later, it was to become his only mean of survival.

****

Whatever had been reported in the Oxnard Courier was clearly not on Emanuel's mind after the Los Angeles wedding. Far from setting off to a homestead in Northern Canada, Irene and Emanuel remained in Los Angeles. If either he or Irene, through her first husband, had been granted land by the Canadian government, I have been unable to find any record. Perhaps, Emanuel had just issued a convenient statement to the press pending other ideas. Alternatively he had been confronted with a lifetime decision to pursue an ambition, a dream to become an Osteopath, or to spend the rest of his life on the harsh lands of northern Canada. His choice was to pursue osteopathy, a singularly American development in medicine. The easy mistake here is to compare medical training, osteopathy and accreditation today and assume that it was more or less the same during the 1920s. Nothing could be further from the truth. To understand the obstacles in Emanuel's path to qualification, it may help to know a little historical background.

Nineteenth century American medicine was wholly unregulated at a national level. This in turn led to some dubious personalities describing themselves as doctors and prescribing totally unsuitable, if not sometimes lethal, drugs. Great progress had been made during the American Civil War of 1861-65 and some of the medical institutions on the east coast matched the best of Europe. The problem remained in bringing medicine to the provinces in the west and far west where isolated populations were reliant on lesser trained individuals. Something had to be done. In 1910, the Carnegie Foundation sponsored Abraham Flexnor, an educationalist, to publish a report about medicine in the United States. It was scathing and commented fiercely on low admission and graduation standards then being achieved by some American doctors. The whole medicine discipline was unregulated, he said, yet to be validated and full of, 'snake-oil-salesmen' with their miracle cures. A doctor's training could be as little as two years and the schools that trained them might have been set up by doctors who themselves had only received a minimum of education. There were simply too many of these low quality schools which produced dubious doctors who degraded the profession. The consequence of the Flexnor report was that during the 1920's, Canada and the United States saw progressive changes for the better in the organisation of medical training and the accreditation of qualifications. But in the early 1920s, when my father began his training, there was a prevalence of the 'old' type doctors and their 'snake oil' still in circulation and legally practising. Into this partially regulated melange of medical practice came the osteopaths. At first nobody quite knew if they were snake oil salesmen, or real doctors.

Osteopathy owes its existence and acceptance to Doctor Andrew

Taylor Still who in 1874 was living on the Missouri frontier. He uncovered, so he said, the significance of living anatomy in health and disease. That is to say that he realised that optimal health is possible only when all the tissues and cells of the body function together in harmonious motion. He reasoned that disease could have its origins in slight anatomical deviation from the normal. Furthermore, he could restore health by treating the body with his hands. He named this approach osteopathy. One can imagine on the frontier without the aid of drugs a doctor's only aid were his hands and what they could do to alleviate pain and discomfort.

Clearly my father had been very impressed by what he had seen during WW1 and may also have truly felt that he had been gifted, as many osteopaths say they are, with a deep sensitivity in their hands. Since the war, this new medical science had moved on, but not sufficiently to be recognised by the "establishment". Osteopathy was very much in its infancy and open to criticism and ribaldry from more orthodox medical practitioners as it is today. Nevertheless, my father had realised that his hands were sensitive to what Dr Still described as, 'anatomical deviation'. Under supervision on the casualty boats he had been allowed to undertake basic procedures, encouraged by the doctors. What he now needed was the academic study and practical training to hone and develop those skills in what today we would call a holistic approach to medicine. The problem for him was that he was completely unable to fund the necessary years of full-time study.

Around Los Angeles, just as Abraham Flexnor had earlier described, there were several medical schools where for the cost of a training course and a diploma, the student could study osteopathy to reach the standard of Doctor of Osteopathy (DO), set up his shingle (brass plate) and practise. When, later, in Canada and England my father was challenged about his qualifications, he duly produced his diplomas. The authorities then declared them as unregulated qualifications, accordingly dismissing them. The main teaching institution in Los Angeles at this time was the College of Osteopathic Physicians and Surgeons. There is no record of my father attending that institution or any other similarly named place. However, by the time he began his studies in osteopathy in 1920 a curriculum had been published which he later referred to in court room evidence. This suggests that he did undertake some structured, formal training, but clearly not enough to satisfy Canadian or English validating bodies. The method of study that he chose may also have been unorthodox for obtaining a qualification in medicine.

One of the key problems in raising educational standards in the United States was how to bring education to the masses located miles away from centres of learning excellence. To overcome this, the nation saw the birth of the correspondence courses and distance learning.

Abraham Flexnor 1866 – 1959

Between 1894 and 1926 a rash of osteopathic books had been published as ready references for students who studied by post. Several institutions offered a sandwich course of theory and practical. Perhaps my father fell somewhere between the wholly postal and sandwich course student, but on a part-time basis. In later life, others would comment that my father's medical knowledge was extensive, convincing and professional to the extent that when his children became ill he could discuss their illnesses at length and in depth with the local practitioner. The only conclusion to be made about my father's qualifications is that they were obtained piecemeal overtime and lacked any formal accreditation.

On September 26th 1919 Irene gave birth to their first son who was named David Frederick. By this time Irene and Emanuel had moved from Oxnard and taken up residence in the suburbs of Los Angeles in the pleasant, Pasadena area of District 63 at 209 Brandon Street. This area was close to Glendale and Hollywood and in later years David Frederick would talk to his own children about how Hollywood stars would come and baby-sit whilst father and mother socialised with the Hollywood glitterati. Quite what Emanuel's then connection with the studios was is not clear beyond, perhaps, jobbing work as an extra. However at this early stage in his marriage to Irene there is strong evidence to suggest that his desire for the opposite sex knew no bounds. Some American family records and anecdotes recall a liaison between Mary Pickford, the silent film star, and my father. It is said that amorous letters passed between them at the same time as Miss Pickford was enjoying a relationship with Howard Hughes. What follows may have some bearing on this aspect, although there is certainly no evidence to corroborate the incident in question. As with so much about my father, there was always a grain of truth in what he recounted. He later recounted to my sister Thelma that in the early 1920's he had been stabbed during a fight. The rights and wrongs of this are now lost to history but it is possible that it may have involved money, women or gambling. Gambling in particular was now to play a greater part in Emanuel's life as he sought to provide for his family on a limited income. Whilst Irene was pregnant his need for sexual satisfaction would cause his eyes to wander to other women. He was, after all a charming, perhaps even charismatic person who mixed freely with 'The Stars.' I suspect, however, that the knifing dented his ego somewhat.

On and off for the next five years Emanuel pursued his osteopathic training, mixing crime and academic learning with some honest toil. The later stages of his osteopathic training were to include, so he said, hundreds of hours spent studying dead bodies at seven undertakers in Los Angeles. As gruesome as this sounds, he declared that this was an essential part of the curriculum to understand the anatomy and physiology of the human body. There are no records of when my father completed his training or even if he ever did. All that is known is that Emanuel and Irene lived at several addresses in LA up until 1927. Within this same period Irene gave birth to two more children. Irene Jane was born on November 16th 1920 and Gordon followed on May 30th 1922. They were now a family of five. There is a hidden assumption that with the building of a family unit, life for Irene and Emanuel had become pleasant, conventional and settled. Somehow, it had not. Instead, as the family moved from one lesser address to another they slowly drifted into unspeakable living conditions and penury, finally, in 1927, ending up in the Los Angeles shelter for the poor and dispossessed. More to the point during this period of his life, my father's fascination with cheque book fraud, which started in 1915, was again to dominate his life.

By his own admission from police records my father's main occupation up until 1927 was as a painting contractor for several outlets in the prestigious, Pasadena area of LA. There is some evidence to suggest that in the early days he was quite successful as he mixed home study with work and enjoyed an honest reputation within the trade. Testimonials that he later presented in court confirmed this. Some study, however, had to be taken full time which meant a reduction in his earnings. In order to fulfil the course in anatomical studies, for example, he needed practical experience which included the dissection of cadavers. This entailed taking up employment with undertakers. The wages at one hundred dollars a month were much less than he had been used to. He clearly felt the pinch. Moreover, there were now three children at home with Irene to be clothed, fed and soon to be educated. He was caught on the horns of a dilemma. As early as 1923, unknown to Irene, he gave way to temptation and was drawn back to casual, chequebook fraud in order to sustain his income. He was very successful and it passed undetected for some years.

By early 1925, my father felt both confident and competent enough to begin work as a practising osteopath. Working under the direction of a qualified doctor who had assisted and encouraged him in his osteopathic studies he attended a child with diabetes. The outcome was pleasingly successful. However, the established local doctor became angry at Emanuel's intervention and questioned who the newcomer was? The medical reforms in America following the Flexnor report were now well underway, inclusive of a state register for all practitioners. My father's name was nowhere to be found on this register. Not surprisingly, the practitioner made a formal complaint and my father was duly arrested and sent for trial in Los Angeles.

On May 25th, 1925, the court found my father guilty of violating the Medical Act and sentenced him to ninety days in prison. The question here is that if my father had any real qualification, surely now was the time to produce that accreditation. Alternatively, in America, state laws may vary considerably from one state to another. Osteopathy was still in its infancy and may not have been accepted in California. Thus, any diploma that my father had would have been automatically disregarded. More likely, as we will see from a court case two years later, was that he was still under training, very enthusiastic and perhaps capable but totally unqualified. He had overstepped the mark; an action that he was often to make throughout his life. Now he must pay for it. During the period of his arrest and trial Irene had survived by living in a state hostel with her children. Almost a year to the day later, on May 26th, 1926, my father was in court again, this time for extortion.

The case grew out of alleged physical harm to his son, David, involving a third person(s), which had occurred whilst Emanuel was in prison. In his later defence and a perverse irony, Emanuel said that he tried to obtain money from the 'guilty party' to pay for medical bills incurred as a result of this physical harm to his son. There is some suggestion in later testimony that he posed as a sheriff's deputy in order to exaggerate his position in this matter. The court did not side with Emanuel, although, reading between the lines of the transcripts, it had some sympathy with his plight. At the end of the day, however, no individual can take the law into his own hands. Judge Westover sentenced my father to a further ninety days in jail, but given the dubious circumstances, suspended the sentence if my father left for Canada immediately. He had received a gypsy's warning from the court.

San Diego Court House Circa 1920

After this second court case, (the fourth case heard in the US against my father and if his naval service is included, his seventh appearance in a court of law), the situation at home had not improved, far from it. Irene became ill and required both medical and nursing attention and there were three young children all of whom needed to be supervised and looked after. In late 1927, in an effort to make ends meet and despite the court warning, Emanuel went on a spree, cashing between 20 to 24 bogus cheques within the Pasadena area. Sooner or later he must have realised from his past experience that he would be found out. Perhaps he even wanted this to happen, knowing that the state would then look after his family. Unsurprisingly, on a sunny November day there came a knock on Emanuel's door from detective Lieutenant E D Kopytek from the Highland Park Division Police Station.

The two soon struck up a rapport. Such was the conviviality that they might have been two old friends meeting to discuss the local ball game. Emanuel clearly wanted to unburden himself and admitted that there had been several more instances of fraud, although he could not quite put his finger on the actual figure. My father found it easy to speak to the police lieutenant confessing multiple cheque fraud over the preceding three years or so. Emanuel was charged with five specimen counts of fraud and sent for trial. This was his eighth appearance in court. He would now also have to explain why he had not left for Canada after the last court case, as he had promised.

In order that the new presiding judge could have all the information at his finger tips Mr H C Vinacke, Assistant Probation Officer, was charged to complete the necessary background report on my father. Of course, Mr Vinacke could only report what was on record and what my father had told him. The lies flowed like Victoria Falls in spate. My father described how he was born in Portland Oregon and graduated from Toronto Technical School in Canada. He claimed also to have received a shrapnel wound in the knee and had been awarded a bravery medal and much more besides. It was incredible. After my father's performance of a lifetime, Mr Vinacke was not impressed. In truth, Emanuel was extremely lucky that no connection had been made by the LA court with his first appearance for the same offence in 1916, under the name of Childs. Had there been, and given his persistent record of forgery offences, he would have undoubtedly received a more harsh and lengthy custodial term in prison.

Luck was to be briefly on Emanuel's side when he appeared before the Honourable William S Baird in the Superior Court of the State of California in February, 1927. Despite what my father had said to Lt Kopytek, he initially pleaded not guilty to certain of these counts. Mr J A Holland, my father's defence attorney, wisely recommended that a plea of guilty might be a better option, given the obvious circumstances of fraud. Wasting the court's time, Mr Holland advised, although delaying the inevitable sentence, would ultimately antagonise Judge Baird! Joseph Ryan prosecuted this case as the Deputy District Attorney of Los Angeles County. He had little to say other than the facts of the case which were damning and spoke for themselves.

In later life, Emanuel tried to explain away these court cases by citing that it was to do with "political" matters resulting from his support for a particular party. But that was balderdash and nothing more than a tissue of lies. His only connection with a political party was a brief association with the Ku Klux Klan, hardly something to crow about! What Irene thought or suffered is not recorded other than by anecdotal evidence passed down to her grandchildren. From 1923 onwards, her life and that of her children was indescribably awful. On the one hand she had to burden the shame of all the petty crimes and misdemeanours in which Emanuel had participated and on the other she had to go cap in hand to the state in order to survive whilst he was in prison. But without a true welfare state and no contact with her own family, the option for her and the children to leave Emanuel was simply not tenable. In a plea for clemency, Mr Vinacke highlighted in his report to Judge Baird the, 'appalling squalor and unpleasantness in which Emanuel's wife and children now lived, surrounded by a number of known degenerates.' The picture that he painted was truly sad, worthy of a Dickensian scene of a hundred years before.

Mr Holland's task to represent my father, on the other hand, was a near vertical, uphill assignment. All he could do was to call on the court's sympathy through an impassioned plea of mitigation. As if to show that my father's lapses into crime were but brief and isolated, my father called on several exemplary references including those of former employers and store owners where he had been known and trusted. This contradictory evidence, suggesting my father's honesty and integrity, was in stark contrast to the known facts. In addition, letters testifying to my father's character and good standing were received from some local worthies. The final documentary evidence was presented by Irene in letters written to the court pleading for her husband. She was now living with the children, she said, in a hostel at 141 North Boylston Road in LA. Despite all her privations, and perhaps the appalling way she had been taken for granted by Emanuel, Irene could not have better supported her husband.

The reports set before Judge Baird were heavily loaded with emotion. Despite all the crimes, he had committed, Emanuel was painted as an intelligent, versatile man who handled himself in court, so his probation officer reported, better than many attorneys! It seems that my father developed a penchant for appearing in court and enjoyed the notoriety, or at least the acting. He seems to have viewed court appearances as a theatrical opportunity to star in his own production. He would arrange the court by having witnesses excluded and even to ask for members of the bench to be removed. He became so adept at this stage management that he could hold the court's attention and persuade them. Persuade them he did to the extent that some of the five charges were dismissed. The thoroughness with which my father prepared his own case and the professionalism with which he presented it led Mr Vinacke to conclude in his probation report that the crimes committed by my father were deliberate, well planned and executed. This was, he commented, an intelligent man applying himself to crime. Accordingly, Mr Vinacke did not recommend probation, preferring instead to recommend the full custodial sentence. This man had to be corrected by a term in prison. Emanuel by then must have had real doubts about his future liberty.

Judge Baird was in a quandary; if he confirmed a custodial sentence against my father, it would only exacerbate the situation and bring more pain and disadvantage to the home. It would also stop my father from returning to Canada, relieving Los Angeles of a financial liability for Mitchell and his family. Judge Baird now looked for other positive signs from the court room happenings. As part of his plea and in admitting his guilt and wrong doing, Emanuel had shown remorse and had said that given the opportunity, he would pay back those whom he had defrauded. This, Judge Baird thought was a step forward in admitting responsibility for what he had done.

In his summing up, before passing sentence, Judge Baird turned and spoke forcibly to my father. "As far as I am concerned you are not entitled to any consideration at all. Your past actions and conduct do not justify any consideration!" The Judge was scathing. My father had been found guilty on two counts for which Judge Baird sentenced him to five years in St Quentin Prison on each count, to run concurrently. But Judge Baird had also taken pity on Irene and the children. He announced in his summary, "Now understand Mitchell that you are standing on the threshold of the penitentiary, and your plea, because of your wife and children, will not avail you anymore. It is only by reason of the fact that the children would suffer through your incarceration that I am giving you this chance to make restitution to those whom you have defrauded and to be a better man to your family. Do you understand that?"

"Yes, sir," my father replied.

But there was more. The judge went on to add, "Another thing. One of the conditions is that you shall not go around posing as a pseudo police officer. I will remind you that we have plenty of police officers." He was referring to an earlier occasion when my father had taken the law into his own hands. "You may feel very large and stately and arrogant if you have a star, but one of the conditions of suspending the sentence will be that if you are found with a star on, it will be one of the violations of your suspended sentence and you will have to go to the penitentiary... Now you go to work and make restitution. You have now got your chance; see that you make the best of it. That is all."

"Thank you," my father replied.

Emanuel was released from police custody on February 24th, 1927. In effect he would be on probation for five years, on the understanding that from his earnings at the undertakers, he would pay back his debtors and show that he was a changed man. The court noted that he was presently employed with the Sharp undertaking establishment earning $100 per month. His probation officer would be Mr Vinacke under the supervision of Carl May.

Looking back at the trial today, the implications of the judgement are clear and chilling. Another misdemeanour and it is straight to St Quentin prison for the next ten years or more if police impersonation was included. But fear of prison, or authority at large, was never a deterrent or obstacle in Emanuel's troubled judgement of what to do next. He seemed impervious to his responsibilities as a husband and father. On November 17th, 1928, nineteen months after his release, Carl May notified Judge Douglas Edmonds at the Los Angeles Superior Court that my father had violated his probation by failing to reimburse any of the money owed. Furthermore, following a diligent search by the Sheriff's department, they were unable to ascertain his whereabouts. A warrant was immediately issued for his arrest. My father, as they say, had, 'done a bunk,' absconded.

In reality, soon after the trial, my father had decided to leave LA and pursue other interests. What chance was there, he thought to himself, in starting again where everyone would know his past. It was as we say today a "no brainer." Whilst Irene and family temporarily remained in the hostel my father set off on his next adventure to make quick money. His earlier life as a sailor and experience in Canada and of the Canadian authority had placed him in a good position to join the bootlegging racket importing illicit booze either from Mexico or Canada. My father refers to Mexico as a former work place in later evidence, but he is principally known for the cross-border trade between America and Canada, as Canada would always be a sanctuary for him. From his prison life he had made many contacts. His credibility in and out of St Quentin was impeccable to other crooks; he had no difficulty in being introduced to and becoming involved with racketeers.

Between 1927 and 1929 Emanuel worked studiously out of Mexico and Canada bootlegging booze into the United States by ship and road. Conveniently, boats frequently sailed from Seattle either to Mexico or to Canada. To be in the right location at the right time, Emanuel moved his family from LA to Oregon and thence to Seattle. There is also a good guess that at the same time his weaknesses for women and gambling were also indulged, although this has to be speculation.

The anecdotal evidence is that for most of this time the family were dodging from one house to another whilst Emanuel involved himself in booze running from Canada or Mexico. He would often be away from home for weeks at a time whilst Irene waited for that knock on the door that would spell Emanuel's incarceration in prison for a very long time. Rum-running and border jumping particularly thrived along Blaine's shared coastline with British Columbia. I can only surmise that from his Royal Navy experience Emanuel had become familiar with that coastline. For nearly two years Emanuel ran the gauntlet between the law and the mob. It is an understatement to say that these trips were dangerous. But that was only half the story. There were always competing turf wars amongst the bootleggers and willingness on behalf of the gangsters, the American Federal and local police to open fire with minimal warning based on the caution of, shoot him before he shoots you. Emanuel could not win. If he crossed the mob there was a bullet; if he crossed the police there was the same; it was the classic no win situation.

At last, sensing the precariousness of his circumstances, something had to change. Irene was at her wits' end and the children were clearly suffering the neglect of a father and a lack of continuity of education, let alone a stable home life. In late 1928 prompted by Irene and the realisation that his life had no value as a bootlegger, Emanuel made the decision to move back to Canada. In early January 1929 and with a wallet once more filled to capacity, thanks to bootlegging, the family moved from Oregon to Vancouver by sea. Their new residence was in the up market area of South Vancouver at 5910 Rupert Avenue, a most respectable suburb. Ironically, it was not far from his old Royal Navy stamping ground at Esquimalt. He breathed a sigh of relief. He was now on familiar territory. It was here that he decided to start his life all over again, but this time as the new American trained doctor. There was, just, one problem. The name Mitchell was tarnished and carried a criminal record which, if the Canadian authorities conferred with their counterparts over the border, would send him straight back to at least a ten-year prison sentence in the US. In an effort to lose his past identity and now probably hiding from the mob, the Royal Navy Police and US police, my father now re-invented himself as Dr E.F.M. Thomas, as his plate informed the unknowing, he was a Physician and Surgeon. Thomas, you may remember was Irene's maiden name.

Who then fingered him; someone from the mob, the medical establishment, a scorned woman… is again unclear, but his cover was soon blown. In truth, his cover story would always be his Achilles heel despite his Oscar level acting ability and easy charm. When the Canadian Police arrested him in May 1929 under the Medical Practice Act, despite his protests at having received a university education, he had neither the oral or written communication skills that might validate such an education. He may have come close to affecting the desired image, but on closer examination, rather like Shaw's Eliza Dolittle, the lax grammar of his speech and written work would always let him down. Furthermore, the lack of accredited qualification or diploma would simply confirm the fraud. My father was duly charged with, "obtaining money under false pretences whilst practising as a Physician & Surgeon". He was sentenced to six months hard labour at Oakalla Prison Farm, Deer Lake, British Columbia. Irene would again be on her own and would once more have to resort to state help for herself and the children.

Vancouver as my father knew it in 1913

Emanuel weathered the prison sentence reasonably well, incurring just the odd hiccup. There was an incident involving the possession of contraband and another involving the use of threatening language to a Mr McLeod and Mr Coppin, both guards at Oakalla Prison. But for the most part he seemed to have knuckled down and behaved himself. Judging by what was to follow, I think that he also took this occasion to open his heart to the Canadian authorities. He was now in his thirties and clearly could not go on stumbling through life. Fate, he thought, had brought him back to Canada. As for Irene, her love and devotion for Emanuel, not to mention loyalty, seemed to know no bounds. Despite all that she had been through, she stuck by her man. Once more she wrote letters to the court to support her husband's pleas. How she maintained her dignity and kept the family together remains one of the wonders of this story. During his six month prison sentence Irene visited Emanuel no less than nine times. A task made all the more difficult as she and her children were accommodated at a government hostel several miles away in Vancouver at 3466 Kingsway. My father was released from Oakalla Prison on November 15th, 1929 with $8.20 in his pocket; a sum earned for good conduct.

Oakalla Prison

In a still later court case that spawned dramatic headlines, the prosecution was to say that my father had been deported from Canada. Although this was to be sometime ahead, it may help to explain the background to this accusation at this juncture. Such a strong statement clearly implied that my father was an undesirable, professional criminal. Although this was true to some extent he had only been in trouble with the Canadian police on the one occasion. What had happened in the United States was as yet unknown to the Canadian authorities. To try and understand the truth behind his repatriation to England we return to a bizarre twist in my father's story relating back to his army life.

When Emanuel was discharged from the Canadian army in 1919, the records indicate that the discharge was gained on medical grounds. These grounds amounted to a knee injury which Emanuel states, 'happened whilst playing football in 1911 in San Francisco'. (This was a lie of course, because in 1911 he was working as a farm labourer after leaving the workhouse for farmer Druford. Nearer the truth may be that the injury was sustained, if at all, whilst undertaking his recruit naval training in 1912.) Emanuel was to say that his service in the Canadian army exacerbated this injury causing permanent damage. He now began a claim against the Canadian Army from his prison cell either prompted by the prison authorities, or just by idle gossip.

The Canadian National Health and Pensions authorities opened a full investigation which resulted in a report and recommendations. This report compared the 1919 account with the second examination conducted at Oakalla, now ten years later. The report included an x-ray assessment. The report found little evidence of a serious injury and no evidence of a wired kneecap being present on the x-ray, although the term "wired" may have referred to some form of gut stitching that had dissolved over time. Nevertheless, the report concluded that there certainly was some disability within his knee joint that would limit his walking ability.

If this knee injury had been as a result of service in the Royal Navy and had been proven and accepted as such, it might have been subject to a British, Admiralty pension award. What a cruel irony. For obvious reasons, Emanuel could not disclose his naval service to the Canadian authorities. He had, after all, deserted from the Royal Navy in early 1914 and if he disclosed this, he would automatically be handed back to the Royal Canadian Navy Police as a deserter! It was what we now know as the classic "Catch 22 situation."

There followed a long sequence of correspondence between Ottawa and Oakalla prison during Emanuel's six months incarceration that ultimately defined his future. Mr G H Sedger was appointed by the Canadian Government as Emanuel's "Soldiers' advisor". He searched through all the available information held by the Canadian Military records and represented Emanuel's interests to the authorities, including his desire not to return, or be returned to the USA. What the result of this representation was remains confidential and under wraps, but there is enough circumstantial evidence to put together a reasoned account. The authorities in Ottawa may or may not have had wind of Emanuel's troubled life in Los Angeles; after all, Emanuel always claimed that he entered Canada direct from Mexico. None the less, realizing that Emanuel was trouble and a liability, the authorities in Ottawa will have viewed the situation that now confronted them as an opportunity for skilful administrative action to rid them of a troublesome individual. The solution put forward would also clear up any ongoing pension liability for an aggravated injury. In short, Emanuel was offered a one-way ticket to England for himself and family, paid by the authorities. He accepted the deal. On November 15th, 1929, after being released from prison, the Mitchell family, escorted by an Immigration Inspector, left British Columbia by rail for Montreal where the family were to board the Liner, RMS Duchess of York bound for Southampton, England.

The preceding nine years that had started with so much excitement, hope and personal confidence had degenerated into a life of hustle, cheating, womanising and forgery. Emanuel had shown himself to be challenged in his ability to see right from wrong and to fail to understand what responsibility or integrity meant: especially the responsibility to his new family. He consistently put himself first with an overblown appreciation of his own abilities. He was bright and quick witted, but he did not have the honed, accumulated and developed skills that made his judgement balanced or shrewd. Today we would describe him at best as a Walter Mitty, or at worst a con man. He pretended to be a doctor in one guise and a policeman with a star on his chest in another. He yearned for recognition. He clearly liked the idea of personal prestige and power and sought an authoritative position over others. His best performance seemed to come when he needed money. He would adopt the persona of a confidence trickster, bullshit his unwitting prey with his silver tongue, finally handing them forged cheques hoping that he would not be caught. How many times he did this has not been recorded, but there is little doubt that he was a serial fraudster and was only prosecuted for a fraction of his crimes. As a result of the 1927 forgery case, we know that in addition to many other aliases, we can now add those of Charles B. Parks, Henry Bainbridge, and F.J. Maloney.

The shy, diminutive, inarticulate workhouse-boy with a heavy Devon accent and a very basic education was now able to hold his own in conversation with professionals and be accepted as a self made man. He could pass himself off as something he wasn't with flair and élan. His time at the acting studios had provided him with the polished tricks of the trade. But his *piece de resistance* was to finally pass himself off as a doctor of osteopathy and remarkably, achieve success in this discipline. In terms of courage, he feared no one and no authority. He dodged bullets from the mob and police alike whilst he bootlegged booze across the US/Canadian border. Whenever the Police caught him, he simply embroidered stories to obtain sympathy from the law. As a father, parent and husband, he had shown himself to be utterly selfish, shying away from responsibility at every turn and devoid of conscience. He was in short, a rogue, a liar, a cheat and a survivor of some accomplishment. There is no more pleasant way of describing him. But his wife loved him dearly and followed him through all of the troubles, always hoping that he would turn the corner into honesty and success.

Fate would now provide my father with a further chance to make good and settle his family in the land of his birth. It had been sixteen years since he left England, just under half his then lifetime. He was now a man with responsibilities who had experienced hard labour in prison. Would this be the turning point in his life? The future was up to him.

Notes

Oakalla Prison Farm at Deer Park closed after WW2 to become the site for new condominiums. The shared strip between Blain and British Columbia became the most used western access for contraband alcohol during the years of American Prohibition.

Chapter 6

Return to the Fold

As the SS Duchess of York entered the Solent on November 30th 1929, the Isle of Wight came into view through a grey, murky sky. Emanuel, Irene, David, Gordon and Irene-Jane, who was now called Jennie, stood on deck huddled together, buffeted by the cold wind and spume being blown off the choppy water. The weather was both cold and depressing. Light sleet hit their faces like tiny pin pricks forcing them to close their eyes tight as the ship turned into wind to enter the harbour. It was hardly the most inspiring of mornings and Irene felt a sense of dread in the pit of her stomach that things would never be right again. Emanuel tried to put a brave face on matters and really wanted to talk about his time in the Royal Navy. How he had sailed from Portsmouth through the Solent on HMS New Zealand and how wonderful England would be. But he couldn't. That would mean opening another 'can of worms' in front of his children and this was neither the time nor the place to add to what already was a depressing situation. To make matters worse, he was not quite sure what would happen when they landed. They had no money to speak of and nowhere to go. In Canada, before leaving, the Mitchells had been told that they would be expected in England and that someone would be there to help them, but that was all.

SS Duchess of York

The Duchess of York was a new ship for the Canadian Pacific line, serving the route from Montreal, via Quebec to Southampton and finally on to Antwerp. She had only been launched in 1928 and everywhere there was a smell of newness and fresh varnish on the wood. The third class accommodation provided by their ticket was sparse but comfortable enough, where the whole family shared one cabin. The Atlantic sea voyage had been rough in the winter seas. Jennie had been especially seasick and had remained in their cabin for much of the eight-day crossing. The atmosphere throughout the journey had been tense between Emanuel and Irene and it showed in their sullen faces. The worry and anxiety of the past months in Vancouver, Oakalla and finally Montreal had placed great stresses on their relationship. Irene had been left wondering if any good would ever come of their marriage. She was also concerned at Emanuel's lack of fatherly example to his children. The ocean crossing had been the first time that they had all been in each other's close company for so long. Emanuel soon grew impatient with the boys and it showed. As always in these matters, the children pick up the tension between their parents and hold these memories for life. Irene had done her best to hold the family together through all of Emanuel's absences and although he had provided some money, the stigma of the way in which it was earned offended her upbringing of Christian honesty. She also felt deep shame for her husband's repeated prison sentences.

As the Duchess of York made her way to her moorings, Emanuel caught a glimpse of Irene and still marvelled at her great attractiveness, although the demanding life that she had been forced to live had hardened her personality. Her eyes looked tired and her face drained. Emanuel was aware that he was impatient with the boys and lacked that fatherly presence that he knew would be essential if they were not to go the same way as him. In consequence, he had a tendency to overreact, when all he meant to do was to steady the situation. He had been far too quick to cuff the boys around the ears or shout abuse at them when really patience and understanding were required. There is no greater gift that a father can give to his children than time and attention. Emanuel had not been there for his children when they needed him most, yet he felt little personal guilt. When he had made his riches he would make it up to them, he argued to himself in his bizarre, befuddled corrupted brain.

Irene now had to acknowledge that Emanuel was different; very different from the army sergeant she first saw resplendent in his uniform with the world at his feet. At the start it was fine. There were those heady days in Pasadena; the Hollywood parties and a promising career in osteopathy to look forward to. But all too soon the dream had been shattered into a bare existence. In the past few years, during tense evenings alone she had agonised as to whether Emanuel would return from bootlegging booze from Mexico or Canada. What would she do if he did not return? He would often be away for several days at a time, out of contact. She knew that during these forays he would spend some of his ill-gotten money on gambling or other women, but what could she do? She was wholly dependent on him and rued the day that she lost her independent, widow's pension. To make matters worse, with three hungry children to feed, she was never sure what there would be for housekeeping. She dreaded the knock on the door. Would it be a policeman or customs official to arrest him, or someone from the mob!

The last time Emanuel returned from one of his cross border forays with young David in tow, bullets had hit the car. David and

Gordon had told Irene of father shouting at them to lie down on the back seat whilst he sped away. David, who was sworn to secrecy by his father not to talk to his friends, found it exciting beyond measure; 'just like the flicks.' Irene was sick and distraught with worry, her hands and body trembling as she listened to the tale. How could Emanuel place the boys in such danger? Irene was not one to throw public tantrums, or to quarrel and row in front of the children. Her sensitivities were far too advanced for that. She would undoubtedly have been a bundle of nerves, but her self-restraint would have controlled her until she was alone with Emanuel. Then, from deep in her heart she would strike with the anger and spite of a cornered, tormented animal. Emanuel would be stunned into silence remaining speechless and cowed in the presence of someone whom most of all he had learned to respect, but never quite enough.

The moment would pass and Emanuel would put the money on the table. Without lifting her eyes from Emanuel, Irene would scoop up the money and stuff it in her bra' (budge) knowing full well that he would never dare touch her and the money would be safe from petty gambling. Deep down, for all Emanuel's philandering and antics, she still loved him. He had the gift of the gab and at heart he was a kind man, but he did not know how to be sensitive or thoughtful. At his best Emanuel was witty and amusing and could always bring a smile to her face. She knew too that he really loved the boys. But, he had no model to follow as to how to treat or nurture them. He favoured Irene-Jane because he was a ladies' man and found female company easy to manipulate. Perhaps most of all Irene realised that Emanuel was a dreamer; she wanted so much to be part of that successful dream.

At Southampton docks, the preliminaries were brief. If there was any interest regarding Emanuel's earlier desertion from the Royal Navy, it was not obvious. Christmas was approaching and some festive decorations were evident around the passenger terminal welcoming new arrivals. The police and customs officials were already aware of the Mitchell family's arrival from information wired from the police in Ottawa. As far as the British authorities were concerned, the Mitchells were returning to England from Canada of their own free will. It was also clear from the information provided by the Canadian authorities that they were likely to be without funds.

After disembarking, the police and immigration authorities waved the family through to be met by the local authority welfare official. Once more, Emanuel would have to place himself and his family at the mercy of the State and seek "poor relief" or in other words, ask for admission into the workhouse.

On the evening of November 30th, 1929, Emanuel, Irene and the three children were admitted into the Southampton workhouse. Built in 1867 to accommodate two hundred and fifty inmates, it was an imposing red brick building with the usual tower at its centre and accommodation wings either side. There were two floors each with large, Georgian, twelve pane windows evenly spaced across the façade. Close by, an extensive Infirmary had been added in 1902 to accommodate the ever-mounting number of older people being abandoned to Parish charity. This workhouse was a much bigger affair than the one at Holsworthy, Emanuel thought, and far more impersonal.

As the Mitchells entered through the heavy oak door, they were met by the smell of still, damp air, scented with disinfectant. Having rung the bell marked, 'please ring for attention', they waited patiently in the entrance hall listening to the sound of tired coughing and shuffling feet in the distances. A dim light from above, purposely placed over the arrivals counter, lit them against their dark surroundings. They were a sad huddle with Jennie clinging to her mother's skirt. The boys said nothing, both now stunned into silence. The situation for the Mitchell family was grim beyond belief. Christmas was coming and at this time of love, compassion and happiness, the family were about to be split up in accordance with the firm institutional rules that Emanuel knew only too well from his Holsworthy days. Amidst tears of the most abject sadness, Emanuel was separated from Irene and the children separated from them both. The children's pleading cries for their mother filled the air. Tears rolled down their faces as they were forcibly taken away. Irene could not look and turned her eyes to the ground sobbing bitterly, her tears forming round, dark droplets on the cold, grey tiled floor. Emanuel tried to comfort her by saying that it would not be for long, but Irene had little faith anymore in anything Emanuel said. The children's wailing ended as a heavy oak door closed behind them as they were led through to another area of the workhouse. The sound of the closing door with its final slam remained in the air for what seemed like several seconds, echoing down the corridor. And then there was silence.

Southampton Workhouse

On December 2nd 1929, for reasons unknown, but likely that the stress, loss of contact and just personal misery was too much for each to bear, the family were discharged from the workhouse at their own request. Where they went is not known, but more than likely to the local Salvation Army hostel. But that could only ever be a temporary expedient. Two days later, on December $4^{th,}$ they were re-admitted back into the workhouse. The reality was that they could not survive without institutional support. They must return to the workhouse for as long as it took for Emanuel to re-establish himself. Of course, the workhouse would try to help with work placements to ease its own burden, but the Mitchells had to resolve themselves to a long stay. Moreover this was 1929, the year of the great stock market crash. Finding work was as rare as finding rocking horse dung. On admission Emanuel had described himself as a painter and decorator, later adding that he was also an electrician. He gave his last known Canadian address as Kingsway, Vancouver BC.

Three days later on December 5th, 1929, after being re-admitted to the workhouse by Mr Luker who was titled a Receiving Officer, David, Jenny and Gordon were 'discharged into the Hollybrook, Borough Children's Home'. Hollybrook House had been specially purchased by the workhouse guardians in 1910 to be used as a home for 150 destitute boys and girls. Twenty years later not much had changed except that the facility had been increased to include several additional cottages for the overflow of impoverished children needing support. It was a comfortable, disciplined facility where the food was regular and wholesome. At least David, Jennie and Gordon would be with children of their own age and able to mix and communicate their anxieties. For Irene the loneliness without the children, segregated from Emanuel, must have been hell personified. The Southampton workhouse could only ever provide temporary accommodation for the Mitchells as my father originated from Holsworthy. The rules were that you went back to your "home" county to be looked after. The Southampton Board of Governors contacted Holsworthy Union on December 10th to ask them to accept financial responsibility for the Mitchells pending their return to Holsworthy. This was accepted in principal, but not immediately. Emanuel would have to find work, or at least try to find work in the intervening period until Holsworthy could receive them.

Hollybrook House Children's Accommodation

My father, as the reader will gather by now, was as ever unpredictable, or was he? I suspect that from the moment that he elected to return to England he had a plan in mind. I also think that he had access to more money than he admitted to the authorities. His actions now speak clearly. On January 8th 1930, he discharged himself from the workhouse never to return, although Irene and the children were to remain 'in care'. The reason that he gave, so he said, was to seek employment and to make contact with members of his west country family and friends. Where he found accommodation and food at this time is unknown although, being a port, Southampton would have welfare accommodation for sailors as well as a Salvation Army hostel. Emanuel melted into the city of Southampton.

True to form, it was not long before he ran into difficulties and as always, the police would be involved somewhere. At Bargate police station, Southampton on January 15th, Emanuel was charged with 'breaking and entering a church.' He gave his Canadian address as 22 Brunswick Square, Vancouver. As always he is never sure how old he is and in one statement he suggests his age to be 33 and in another 36! What he may not have bargained for, but most probably enjoyed the notoriety, was to find himself in the January 18th edition of the 'Hampshire Advertiser and Southampton Times'. Judging by the reported events, it seems that all those earlier court appearances in America and Canada had been quite instructive. When he appeared before Southampton Magistrates he decided to represent himself and take centre stage. The following is taken directly from the newspaper of the time.

Hampshire Advertiser and Southampton Times

January 18th 1930
'NO INTENTION OF HARM
Southampton Charge Dismissed

An able cross-examination by a prisoner of a police officer was a feature of a case heard by the Southampton Borough magistrates on Thursday. The accused man, Emanuel Mitchell (33) described as an electrician, of no fixed address, was charged on remand with breaking and entering the Avenue Congregational Church, on January 8th, with intent to steal. A further charge of being found on enclosed premises, namely a covered out-passage, at the Avenue Hall, for an unlawful purpose on the same date was not proceeded with.

At the outset, the accused, who spoke with an American accent, asked to be furnished with paper and pencil in order that he might take a note of the evidence. He also requested that all witnesses should be ordered out of court. His requests were complied with, and during the hearing of the case he took copious notes.

P.C. Hamblyn stated that when questioned, first the prisoner refused to explain and then said: "Oh well, I'll tell you. I came here to sleep." The prisoner also made a lengthy statement as to what he had been doing for a number of days past. Witness went on to say that he searched prisoner and on him found a spanner, an unemployment book, four keys, a pocket-knife, a pair of gloves, and other things. He took him to Portswood Police Station and there charged him with being found on enclosed premises for an unlawful purpose. The prisoner said he wished to make a statement and it was taken down by Sergeant Cottell.

On January 15 he charged the prisoner (Mitchell) at Bargate Police Station with breaking and entering the church, with intent to steal therein. The prisoner made no reply.

PRISONER'S QUESTIONS
In cross-examination, the policeman said that he went on duty on that particular beat at ten o'clock. The prisoner made no statement to him which he had since found incorrect. He did not see anything on prisoner's clothing indicating that he had tried to climb a wall. He saw nothing which came off the wall on prisoner's gloves. As far as he remembered the spanner was in the prisoner's right hip-pocket. Someone had obviously cut the window cord with a knife. There was not a light in the Avenue which lit up the passage. The window had not been examined for fingerprints.

CANADIAN IDEA

Evidence was also given by Thomas Anglin, 47 Livingstone-road (caretaker at the Avenue Church), and P.S. Cottell. The latter stated that he took down a statement from prisoner at Portswood Police Station, in which the prisoner said he was at present an inmate of the Workhouse, St Mary-street, and an electrician, unemployed. On the night of January 8 he (prisoner) was walking up the Avenue in a northerly direction, and saw the church situated on the right side of the Avenue. He entered the gate for the purpose of finding shelter for the night. Upon entering a dark passageway he heard footsteps coming from the rear. He suddenly became alarmed and started to run, but the person flashed a light and commanded him to halt, which he did. He was somewhat surprised to find that this person was a police officer. He was under the impression that a church was a public institution, and was open to all persons who entered in a lawful manner, that being a recognised rule in the Dominion of Canada. He had absolutely no intention of illegally breaking and entering the church.

The Chairman (Mr R Andrews) stated that the Bench did not consider that the evidence was sufficiently strong, and prisoner would be discharged'.

****

Whatever Emanuel had been up to is not absolutely clear. He may have been looking for something of value to purloin and then sell to a "fence" for cash. Alternatively he may just have been seeking shelter from a cold winter's night. Above all this report gives some idea of the harshness of the times and the struggle that Emanuel had just achieving a winter's night shelter. Between January 8th – the date of the alleged offence-and the date of the hearing in the Magistrates court on January 18th, my father may well have been in custody as he was not then living in the workhouse. Under those circumstances he would be fed and looked after. This begs the question, was his action in being arrested deliberate simply to achieve a bed and food to tide him over? There does seem to be a pattern emerging of such repetitive behaviour throughout his life as he resorts to his survival instinct. On his release from Police custody on January 18th, he once more melts back into Southampton's city life for nearly a month. He must have been feeling very pleased after representing himself in court and being acquitted. His ego had been given tremendous boost. Anything was possible, he thought, all you need are the guts to go for it.

The administrative wheels of the Holsworthy workhouse seemed to turn extremely slowly. It was not until February 17th, just over a month after the church incident, that the paperwork was in place for the Holsworthy Union to accept responsibility for Emanuel and his family. The day before, David, Jenny and Gordon had been released from Hollybrook into the care of their parents. To complete the picture, a Mr Stone had also arrived on that day being the appointed agent to accompany them on their journey back to the Holsworthy workhouse.

The train journey to Holsworthy was uneventful. The third class carriage was cold and bare. The windows were frosted over for most of the journey, thanks to the condensing breath of the family and their fellow travellers on the carriage windows. Nobody said very much. Jennie sat in the corner by the carriage window watching a white, powdery, crystalline shape slowly grow as more condensation ran down the window into the corner and froze. At least the clothing that they had brought from Canada was thick, heavy and warm. Emanuel was deep in thought and had no inclination even for small talk. By now Jennie, bored with the crystals was cuddled into her mother's arms in the corner of the carriage. She had deftly made a port hole in the frosted window and looked out over the Somerset and Dorset countryside as the train made its way steadily through Temple Coomb on to Exeter, before turning north for Holsworthy.

The welcome at Holsworthy was matter of fact, offhand and demeaning. Once more the family were split-up and both Irene and Emanuel felt a deep shame and anxiety for their situation. If Emanuel had anticipated a return home amongst friends and what had sixteen years ago been his family, he was to be quickly disabused. As far as the authorities at Holsworthy were concerned, Emanuel had no credibility or standing whatsoever; he was just another failure and burden on society. Nevertheless, there was one faint ray of hope on the horizon. The workhouse had quickly found Emanuel work on the local railway. It was only manual work, but it would help reimburse the Union expenses for bringing his family to Holsworthy and perhaps help him start again.

From later accounts, Emanuel described the work at Holsworthy as hard, pick-and-shovel exertion on the cold Devon hillsides shovelling granite chips under sleepers, clearing drains and trimming banks. Otherwise, for the moment, all the children were placed in school locally and Irene did her best to weather the circumstances. The Headmistresses school diary indicates the arrival of the Mitchell family from America as "an exciting event" in this rural community. Excitement was hardly the description on Irene's mind. Deep down in that troubled mind of his, Emanuel was still being driven by his dream of practising osteopathy. How much he had declared to Irene about his future intentions is not known, or indeed if she shared his enthusiasm. Perhaps for her it was just a case of hoping that all the pain would stop and some kind of normal life would resume. I suspect that the biggest problem that confronted their future plans was, as before, to have sufficient funds. One can imagine Irene, having seen it all before in Vancouver, and Los Angeles, raising her eyes to the heavens and uttering under her breath, 'in God's name, not again, where on earth will the money come from?'

Emanuel was nothing if not quick-witted. In some respects, he may have been a man before his time. Recognising that on arrival at the workhouse the treatment he and his family had received was less than friendly, he tried his hand at an angry letter requesting compensation. Quite what the problem was has not been recorded, but board of governors certainly considered 'a letter' of complaint from him. In a follow up statement the board recorded that his complaint had been "accepted". Quite how much he was paid remains unclear, but Irene's prayers would be answered. Events now take a Herculean leap forward.

By the late spring (April/May) of 1930, less than four months after arriving destitute at Southampton docks, there was a spectacular change in my father's fortunes. The impoverished, workhouse accommodated Emanuel Mitchell, bootlegger, painter, decorator and sometime electrician was suddenly transformed over night into: Dr E F Mitchell, Physician and Surgeon. Even more staggering was that he had arranged and rented consulting rooms at 54 Treville Street, Plymouth-telephone number: Plymouth 3591. He had positioned himself at the very head of professional respectability. It was, of course, a repeat of the Vancouver, Dr Thomas scam, but it was worth a try. In short, grasping destiny with both hands Emanuel had set up in medical practice using his compensation gains which he may or may not have compounded with the help of a little gambling. Much later, Chinese whispers suggested that he had also been staked by a well-to-do woman, but that would not become public for some time. If this were to be true, his silver tongue and charm had once more delivered him in to the arms of a willing mistress who would satisfy his desires (Irene was pregnant again!) and fill his wallet at the same time. By any account this was a superlative achievement for a now accomplished trickster. It could not have been better. On the one hand he had credible "arm candy" with money and on the other, his consulting rooms and home were located right at the heart of Plymouth. Emanuel had successfully re-invented himself....again.

Irene David Jennie & Gordon Circa 1930 England
(Irene bore a considerable likeness to my mother)

Treville Street was composed of interlocking terraced properties. At street level these properties had been constructed as double fronted shops with a central door set back to allow plate glass viewing areas either side, before entering the shop. Although by today's standards these premises were modest, the bonus was the living accommodation on the level above. In short, it was an ideal location for consulting rooms on the ground floor and family accommodation above. How well or otherwise the children adapted to this change in circumstances has not been recorded. Available records indicate that they were enrolled in Oxford Street School off Mutley Plain, perhaps a half an hours walk from Treville Street. Given all the turbulence in their lives the children did well to hold their own at school. I doubt that Emanuel had given time to consider the importance of continuity in his children's education. Any thanks for that must go to Irene.

So it was that Dr Mitchell began practising as an osteopath. Irene represented the 'front of house' and conducted patients to see the doctor. Business blossomed. Within a short period of time my father had established his practice and managed to forge a comfortable living with a growing reputation as the 'new' doctor from America. His willing mistress had her own property and fortunately for him, her husband was more inclined to Free Masonry duties in the evening, than serenading his wife at home. Given this situation, Emanuel was only too pleased to fill the gap carrying out evening calls at their house.

The lady in question was Lenora Congdon wife of Henry Congdon a Tax Inspector from Stoke, a rather poor area of the Devonport-Plymouth conurbation. Lenora, on the other hand, was the only daughter of a well-to-do and respected yeoman farmer from the Bridestowe, a small, parochial village on the southern edge of Dartmoor. She was bright, cheery and before she married, had a reputation as being charming and amusing company. Like most girls of her time, she left school at fourteen and for a while had been employed by Lord Carrington's household working as a 'tweeny' (in between) maid. Lord Carrington's estate was near to her family's farm called Cranford. Her father, Sidney John Reep and her mother, Elizabeth Kate, were stalwarts of the local area. Although a tenant farmer, Sidney John came from a long line of successful Devon farmers and had an enviable reputation as a fair employer and "good" all round man. He was also widely read and held considerable sway in the community. Most of all he was a pillar of the village, Methodist Chapel.

Elizabeth Kate, however, was altogether a different kettle of fish. She was narrow-minded and nervy with little humour in her life. The Reep family of the 1920's were a family clinging on to the vestiges of a long Victorian and shorter Edwardian heritage. They found it difficult to understand the new, liberated youth of 'flappers' and the desire of all to smoke and consume alcohol. For them, being seen as upright in the community was paramount. There had to be a place for everything and everything neatly in its place, particularly where outsiders might observe. Elizabeth Kate was understandably protective of Lenora, her only child. My mother's upbringing was strict, but fair, so she would tell us. She was urged and encouraged to seek what qualification she could and to embrace the chapel. For most of her young life she had a lonely existence away from children of her own age. Cranford was a farm two miles or so from Bridestowe village, edging on the cold, but beautiful slopes of Dartmoor. Home life at Cranford consisted of routine farm work and little play. The imposed high spots in her life centred on Chapel functions or attending Tavistock pannier market to sell butter and cream churned at home and sold to provide a weekly cash flow. Most of all, however, my mother excelled at singing. She gained considerable acclaim as a choir soloist during an era when touring church choirs were an essential village and small town entertainment. Her singing achieved considerable success and was rewarded by Royal School of Music acknowledgement. It also gained for her a retinue of male admirers with whom she would flirt and tease.

Behind that Victorian veneer of Chapel virtue was a repressed, bubbly character, desperate for fun and someone who loved the attention of young men. Lenora was articulate, extremely good looking even winsome when it came to attracting the opposite sex. Even to this day, those who remember her cannot help but comment on her vivacious character often stringing two or three young men along at the same time and event! How much Sidney John and Elizabeth were aware of this is not known, but I believe that they were conscious that their daughter was single minded, bright and determined with considerable drive and energy. They may also have been aware that although she enjoyed country life, becoming a farmer's wife was not an option that she wanted to consider. Although this is supposition, I believe that having seen life at Lord Carrington's Estate, albeit from below stairs, and perhaps having been wooed there, she sought more from life than the drudgery of a moorland farmer's wife. In 1928 my mother celebrated her twenty third birthday and I suspect was experienced in the ways of the world. For some time, an older, respected official had been visiting Cranford on tax matters. His name was Henry Congdon.

Henry Congdon, who preferred to be called Harry, was a civil servant from Plymouth. He had become a regular visitor to Cranford on government tax business over past years. He offered an air of authority and respectability and behind the rather bland exterior was a personable, well mannered man with good looks. He had served his country in WW1 and like most veterans spoke little about his experiences. More to the point, he had shown considerable interest in Lenora, returning out of business hours to court her. Perhaps it was his modesty combined with his secure employment and good prospects that appealed to Sidney John and Elizabeth. To Lenora, he was a widely travelled man of the world, older than her and the one who held the key to a new life away from Cranford. It would be nice to think that their love and passion for each other knew no bounds. But I have sneaking doubts. I think that it was more a marriage of convenience where my mother knew that she would have the upper hand in the arrangement.

Close friends who knew my mother at the time said later that she married to escape the tedium of home life. Harry was just a convenient conduit. In her romantic assignations before Harry, Lenora had found it easy to manipulate her suitors on a level similar to Scarlett O'Hara in 'Gone with the Wind.' In later life, my mother was rarely without a man on her arm who had not succumbed to her charms. But conversely, she could not tolerate a fool or idler. On the other hand, Harry was ready to settle down. He had found and wooed, so he thought, an excellent catch coming from a respectable moneyed family. He was seven years my mother's senior, from a vastly different, urban and more working class background and at age twenty-nine was approaching the pipe and slippers stage.

Lenora and Harry were married in Bridestowe Methodist Church on September 5th 1928. Sidney John and Elizabeth provided Lenora with a magnificent send-off and generous allowance. Whatever my mother expected to follow, or what Harry had led her to believe, soon became a bitter disappointment. All at once my mother found herself in an ill-equipped, poorly maintained, rented flat close to Harry's family in the distressed area of Devonport. This was so different from the wide open spaces of Dartmoor with the freedom to come and go as she pleased and always a warm farm house to return to at the end of the day. She missed too the animals, especially the dogs that had been her confederates and companions during those lonely years at home. All too quickly the marriage moved into an uneasy routine of my mother being a housekeeper and Harry expecting his washing done, his supper on the table at 6.30 pm, followed by bed, roll over and tomorrow would be another day, exactly the same.

On many evenings Lenora would be left alone in unfamiliar surroundings bored and frustrated. Harry, on the other hand, saw his priority as attending Masonic Lodge meetings to improve his chances of promotion at work and his standing in the community. It becomes an all too familiar story which sees tension rise where the one cannot understand the attitude taken by the other. They quickly grew apart.

To Sidney John and Elizabeth Reep's joy, in March 1929, Lenora became pregnant. Sidney and Elizabeth delighted the couple by giving them, or more explicitly, giving Lenora, a terraced house in the respectable Plymouth suburb of St Budeaux. Sidney John had always considered their daughter's flat unfit to raise a child. My mother's first daughter, Thelma, the only issue from the marriage with Harry, was born on November 12th 1929. Soon after, Lenora, Harry and Thelma moved to the new house at 16, Victoria Villas, St Budeaux, a bay fronted terraced building not far from Saltash and Brunel's famous bridge over the river Tamar. In the other direction lay the temptations, bright lights and excitement of Plymouth.

The only information about my mother's brief marriage, although it legally lasted twenty-eight years, is anecdotal. In essence, it is said that Lenora found Harry dull and argumentative, his Latin roots, so Thelma later explained to me, betraying a terrible temper. He was not going to give in to the single minded and selfish Lenora despite the fact that she had her own money and allowance. She would have to accept their situation and that Free Masonry ranked high in his priorities.

Lenora, by comparison, was not going to be lectured to by a jumped up civil servant in an apron, no matter that the apron alluded to his Free Masonry! Her petulant temper-tantrums were also the stuff of later legend. She could be impatient and quick to rise at what she saw as being unfair or wrong. As if to reinforce her position she would impose her loud voice often leading to physical blows. Her intimidating persona and quick temper made her a feared woman throughout her life. It took a brave and determined man to stand up to her. Most of all, as an only child, she was used to having her own way. From the birth of Thelma onwards her marriage to Harry went steadily downhill. So much so that by 1932, Harry had been ejected from the marital home, or had simply fled unable to bear my mother's mercurial temper.

As so often happens, it wasn't just a question of compatibility. There was also gossip at the time that during the long days and evenings Lenora was left at home she had taken a lover who would tactlessly park his motorbike outside the house when he called. Others stated that the household rows were so heated and physical that Harry simply had enough and left the marriage voluntarily. But he did not desert Thelma. All through her childhood, he contributed to her education and well being, although my mother refused his wish for her to be educated at a Masonic school. Harry never forgave my mother and only agreed to a divorce twenty eight years later in 1957, when my mother admitted adultery. The marriage was then dissolved.

Such then, were the surrounding circumstances of Lenora and Harry's largely unhappy and distressed married life. Fate was now to take a step in my mother's life which would ultimately turn her existence upside down and estrange her from her father and much else besides.

16 Victoria Villas St Budeaux (2007)

My Paternal grandfather's house at Cranford still stands and the village of Bridestowe is little changed. My mother's house at Victoria Villas was destroyed in the blitz but the next door house which was a mirror version (No 16) remains. Treville Street was wholly destroyed by bombing and no longer exists. Southampton workhouse has now become council buildings along with Hollybrook house. Devonport was very badly bombed during the war thanks to its close proximity to His Majesty's Dock Yard. The same fate fell to the neighbouring St Budeaux. Lord Carrington's son went on to have a distinguished war record in WW2 to later become Foreign Secretary in Margaret Thatcher's government. Devonport remains a much slimmed down naval dockyard specialising in submarine warfare. In English farming there is a distinction between lowland and moorland farmers. Moorland farmers were always considered to be the more earthy as they struggled on poor land often living in poor conditions. Sidney John Reep progressed from being a moorland farmer to become much more of a gentleman, yeoman farmer; a subtle distinction then, but of no consequence now.

Chapter 7

Out of the Frying Pan into the Fire

After Harry Congdon vacated the marital home, Emanuel was to progressively make himself comfortable in Lenora's surroundings as a regular visitor, confidant and lover; but not immediately. The separation between Emanuel and Lenora that led to Harry leaving the home cannot be laid entirely at the feet of Emanuel. If there were problems in Harry and Lenora's marriage, and there seems little doubt that there were, they happened within the early months of their marriage before Emanuel was on the scene. This raises the question, when and how did Emanuel and Lenora get together? There are two scenarios how this might have happened.

Since early childhood Thelma had suffered badly with eczema. For some time my mother had consulted her local doctor only to be prescribed ointments that had a varying success rate. As Thelma approached her second birthday, (1931) the eczema was profound and approaching her eyes. There was real concern that her eyesight could be seriously threatened. Perhaps it was in a doctor's waiting room, or gossip amongst young mothers, or even from Harry himself, but Lenora learned of a new "nature doctor," Doctor Mitchell, who had arrived from America. He had fast gained a reputation with his healing abilities using natural remedies. For Lenora, there was nothing to lose. The doctor's surgery was the centre of town at Treville Street, only a bus ride away and a two minute walk from the Cathedral.

Harry & Sidney John (back), Lenora, Thelma & Elizabeth Kate (1930)
Cranford

It is not recorded if Irene and Lenora ever met, but there is strong circumstantial evidence that they did, as Irene fronted the surgery and no doubt handled the diary, the billing and accounts. She had, after all, been a qualified nurse in Canada and as such would have undertaken first aid and changed the dressings on patients. For Dr Mitchell's practice to have gained so much credibility and popularity in such a short time, it had to be a matter of teamwork with Irene. But there was more. In the treatment of eczema Dr Mitchell was ahead of his fellow local practitioners and creating quite a reputation with his success rate. Dr Mitchell's treatment involved the use of ultra violet radiation. After half a dozen or so consultations Thelma's eczema was very much in decline. Within six months it had gone. Other doctors agreed that it had probably saved Thelma's sight. This first scenario suggests that Lenora and Emanuel were brought together through the treatment of Thelma's eczema sometime around 1931.

Although convenient, it is difficult to view the Thelma-eczema account as the sole explanation. This puts their first meeting as sometime during late 1931. When, several years later Emanuel was asked in court who stumped up the money for the surgery at Treville Street, he readily identified my mother. This suggests a second, more probable account of an earlier meeting. During the period that Emanuel was estranged from Irene after the Southampton court case in the winter of 1930, he had probably made his way to Plymouth on a reconnaissance. It is not too difficult to imagine that whilst killing time in Plymouth, perhaps at North Road station, he accidentally bumped into my mother returning from a visit to Bridestowe. (The events brought to life in 1949 film "Brief Encounter" spring to mind.) Emanuel would have been very impressed, if not excited, by her good looks. In his usual smooth, confident way, he would have engaged her in conversation. For him it would be yet another repeat performance. Lenora, the country bumpkin, would have been flattered by his attention. It is not difficult to expand that version where Lenora offers him a bed for the night which in turn would provide him with the opportunity to seduce her. Over breakfast he would divert her by explaining how he was waiting for funds from Canada for the new Plymouth surgery. Naively, I have no doubt that Lenora would have taken the bait and offered the funds. He was after all a professional in a most distinguished vocation, or so it appeared. If this or something like it was the case, mother could indeed have staked him for the Treville Street Surgery in the spring of 1930. Whatever the scenario, it is absolutely clear that Emanuel was two-timing Irene almost from the moment he arrived on English soil. This is a particularly sad indictment on a man who had betrayed and cast aside the woman who had given him so much love, support and loyalty at Oakalla prison and before.

The situation can be summed-up simply as a lonely Mrs Congdon being gradually taken in by a manipulative con artist, Dr Mitchell. Whilst Thelma was receiving the ultra violet radiation treatment, Dr Mitchell had time to regale Lenora about his colourful past. She would have heard wonderful tales about San Diego and Hollywood, how he had met the film stars and of course his WW1 experiences in the Canadian army. She in return would have discussed some of her relationship problems with Harry and why she was now estranged from him. Increasingly, Dr Mitchell became that soft, sympathetic shoulder to cry on. Lenora at her most vulnerable had walked slap bang into the centre of Emanuel's web of deceit and fantasy.

As the consummate actor and having established a basic relationship with Lenora, Emanuel would have provided accounts of his own relationship with Irene to obtain Lenora's sympathy. He would have told Lenora the tragic news that Irene had lost the child she was expecting when they arrived in England and how after losing the baby, she had become increasingly depressed and withdrawn. But as always he will have missed out the key point. Being a very perceptive woman, Irene will have been aware from past experience that Emanuel was up to his old tricks womanising and probably gambling. There is a sixth sense in women who know when their husbands are cheating on them. The usual symptoms stack up: time spent away from home, late evening calls, lack of sexual appetite at home and finally money problems. These may all have applied to Emanuel at this time. It was also the case that Irene did not like England and for some time had expressed a wish to return to Canada to see her family.

Emanuel, on the other hand, would have summarised and translated the above story as the ideal opportunity for him and Lenora to get together, once Irene had gone. But there was the usual problem; how would he be able to fund the ticket to Canada for Irene and three children? In later court evidence he simply says that he "borrowed it."

If my extremely lonely and gullible mother now saw her future with Emanuel, it would be in her interest to see Irene and the children return to Canada as soon as possible. I believe that, once again, Lenora stumped up the necessary cash. On August 3rd 1932, just over two and a half years after arriving in England, now aged thirty six years, Irene returned to Canada on the Cunard Liner, RMS Ascania. On arrival in Montreal she headed home to Halifax, Nova Scotia and her roots. In addition to the three children who accompanied her, she was once more pregnant with her fifth child. Emanuel had provided a parting gift.

RMS Ascania

No sooner had Irene gone than Emanuel moved into Lenora's house at St Budeaux. Emanuel, the serial adulterer, fraudster, trickster and cheat had triumphed beyond his wildest dreams. To cap it all, business was booming. His patient list had grown to include many of the rich and famous of Plymouth society as well as of Plymouth Argyle football team. In the eyes of many, Emanuel was the epitomé of professional respectability. He was acknowledged as a leader in his profession being often invited by outside groups to give presentations and explanations on a variety of medical subjects. Most of all his various treatments had achieved great success with acknowledgement.

As he was now living with Lenora, he no longer needed the surgery at Treville Street with accommodation above. He quickly began a search for more prestigious premises to match his growing reputation. The new location he chose was the impressive, neo Gothic, Prudential Buildings on Bedford Street in the business centre of the city. Dr Mitchell acquired suite 4 and 5; two lavishly furnished consulting rooms complete with state of the art equipment. Things could not be better. Emanuel was now happily established and increasing his client base every day. His healing powers and drug free treatment had genuinely won him great acclaim. But as always in his life, disaster was never far away.

Once Irene had returned to Canada, family accounting and bill paying fell by the wayside; simply, Emanuel considered it trivia and would get around to paying bills when the 'red letter' arrived. He had far more important things to do. As a result, he was summonsed before the local magistrates on several occasions for the non-payment of minor bills and the council taxes of the time (Rates). In early August 1933, no doubt thinking this was yet another small summons; an official OHMS (On His Majesty's Service) letter arrived on his mat, but this time directing him to appear before Plymouth Magistrates on the 30th of the month. He had been charged, so the letter informed him, on four counts: unlawfully, wilfully and falsely using the title 'Doctor' implying he was registered by law as a practitioner in medicine; unlawfully using the title surgeon, unlawfully using the title physician, unlawfully using a title implying that he was registered under the Medical Services Act of 1858. It was San Diego and Vancouver all over again. The case had been brought against my father by the Medical Defence Union, an organisation for registered medical practitioners.

The case was prosecuted by Mr John Woolland and heard by Magistrates Mr G H Smith and Mr R B Johns. Unsurprisingly, on this his twelfth appearance in a court of law, my father conducted his own defence. True to form, Emanuel recognised one of the Magistrates as someone, a solicitor with whom he had done business, but said he did not mind if Mr Woolland had no objection; he did not. The point against Mr Mitchell was, so Mr Woolland pointed out, that on his brass plate and in the telephone directory, my father had described himself as a "DO". In addition, on his writing paper he used the degree abbreviations, DC, DO, ND, which stood for Doctor of Chiropractics, Doctor of Osteopathy and Nature Doctor. He not only claimed to be an osteopathic physician and surgeon, but his notepaper described that he was a medical adviser to a certain council and a lecturer to another. If the severity of the charge was intended frighten Emanuel, it did not, after all no one had complained about his treatments, quite the contrary. Nevertheless, Emanuel was perplexed as to how this prosecution had come about. But he did not have to wait long to find the answer.

Prudential Buildings in the background 1922

"All of these things may have passed unnoticed," Mr Woolland continued, "had not the defendant, on May 9th written a letter to the Western Evening Herald for publication. The letter dealt at some length with medical matters of such character that would usually be dealt with by a qualified medical practitioner. Mitchell signed the letter, osteopathic physician and surgeon and thus drew attention in the most public way... but his name does not appear in the Medical

Register."

There was no third party to look for. Emanuel had shot himself in the foot. "I am prepared to admit, I am not a duly registered practitioner under the Act". Emanuel replied in an opening statement and then commenced to give a well presented and articulated defence.

The offending letter was all about puerperal sepsis, a disease confined to maternity wards. The letter was a well written medical argument that welcomed a public enquiry into the outbreak of the fever that had occurred at the Three Towns Maternity Home. Significantly, the argument put forward by the Medical Defence Union hinged not on the rights and wrongs of such an inquiry and how it might help in solving the problem, but rather on the medical establishment demanding, 'Who is this man Mitchell; how dare he question us?' It is also clear from my father's letter that his knowledge on the subject was extensive and in this instance, his powers of written expression matched his knowledge.

In his summing-up Mr Woolland made no mention of the point or argument behind the letter simply calling for the maximum fine to be imposed against my father. In defence my father called a number of influential witnesses. All the witnesses claimed that my father never misled them. He had advised councils and he had given lectures. It was all true. As with regard to the term physician and surgeon my father cheekily asked the bench if the British Medical Council had a monopoly over the use of these words and put forward a solid counter argument. To a large extent, my father had won over the court through a persuasive, thoughtful defence. The bench retired for some time to consider his case. When they returned they found him guilty of unlawfully using the term physician and surgeon, just two of the four charges. When Mr Woolland asked for costs, the bench refused, thus showing some sympathy with my father. There was no censure to prevent my father from further practising.

The offending letter my father had written shows that he had extensive medical knowledge with considerable interest in maternity matters; an aspect that was to show itself in a less pleasant light some years later. Nevertheless, he had spotted something that the established medical fraternity thought was better not discussed openly. It is a problem with us today and relates to infection inside the hospital and how to control it. The reverse of the problem was how on earth could all these well paid and distinguished worthies allow it to happen in the first place? (The question we do not ask today!) But that would put the medical establishment under the spotlight and suggest incompetence. That could not, under any circumstances, be allowed to happen. If my father ever did anything right in his life, it was to write this letter to raise public awareness about the risks of hospital infection to pregnant mothers and how there was a need to isolate, identify and clean up. But that was all buried in the court case.

May 9th Edition, 1933

To the Editor, "Western Evening Herald"

Sir,
Many citizens are of the opinion that puerperal sepsis is a disease confined to maternity wards. I may state, after extensive study and investigation, tedious searching of medical files on this subject that the weight of evidence is against the theory.

Dr John C Douglas divides puerperal fever into three species: (1) Synochal puerperal fever; (2) Gastro-bilious puerperal fever; (3) Epidemical or contagious puerperal fever.

The latter specie, he states, is often found in the lying-in wards.

Puerperal sepsis should be easily detected by a hospital staff, and under no circumstances should epidemical or contagious puerperal fever be confused with the first or second species. Dr Douglas is apprehensive that the contagion may be conveyed by persons much engaged in hospital duty at a time when its atmosphere is heavily loaded with this peculiar alluvium.

No institution cares to welcome open inquiries where epidemic diseases have taken many victims; but quoting Sir John Pringle MD FRCS, in a letter to the "Medical Chirurgical Review" on "The care *of the Sick," institutions must always be ready to offer all reasonable assistance in the investigation of deaths under questionable circumstances.*

What is the explanation of the epidemic at Stonehouse? I entirely agree that an inquiry should be public. The committee must not be entirely composed of medical practitioners. The layman must have representation.

The Three Towns Maternity Home has nothing to fear from a fair and impartial public investigation. If anything is concealed from the public in this investigation there are many expectant mothers who will terribly fear motherhood.

EMANUEL F MITCHELL
Osteopathic Physician and Surgeon
Plymouth May 9, 1933

****

From this moment the fortunes of my father and his mistress began the steady decline into real pain and hurt. Although on the face of it Emanuel looked prosperous with his two cars, a beautiful mistress, two dogs and a patient list the envy of many a practitioner, the truth was that the stock market collapse of 1929 had been followed by what we now call the depression, an economic famine that lasted until WW2. To achieve what he did during the years 1930 to 33, in the face of the then economic climate was impressive. Nevertheless, as the depression began to bite into the fabric of the nation, (pretty much as it does today-2010), so his fortunes began to dwindle. Quite how bad matters were can be seen from the following letters which passed between Irene and Emanuel over the next two years.

These letters came to the surface when in January 2007 I met my nephew Marc (the son of Gordon, who was Irene and Emanuel's third child). We meet in Venice, Florida. It becomes clear from these letters that Irene had badgered Emanuel to allow her to return to Canada. There is also a strong inference that because the ticket is one way, it may have been a trial separation at Irene's request. In accepting this state of affairs, Emanuel had made promises to provide some ad hoc funding to help the children.

In March 1934 Emanuel writes to Irene. The time is ten months after the Puerperal Fever case of May 1933 and nineteen months since Irene and the children had left on the RMS Ascania for Canada. The child Irene was carrying when she left had been born and was now just over a year old and named Ronald. Back in Plymouth, business had dropped off in the backlash from the 1933 court case, although in fairness, Emanuel continued to have his circle of admirers and satisfied clients. Unbeknown to Irene however, Emanuel had moved into my mother's house at Victoria Villas soon to openly give the telephone number there as a contact address. Nevertheless, it is clear from this letter that he still held some feelings for Irene and missed his children deeply.

In reproducing these letters, the grammar, punctuation and spelling is exactly as my father wrote them down. This letter and the following example were originally typed or written by hand.

Prudential Buildings
Suite 4/5
Plymouth

March 15th 1934

Dear Irene and Family

Received your two letters OK glad to hear from you, but sorry to hear that Ronald has been poorly. I intended to drop you a line sooner but I have been very poorly myself and could hardly walk, but today I have come out for a few hours.

I have had a bad attack of Rheumatism in the knees and it has been extremely hard to get over with it.

Business is so bad here I am afraid that I will have to give up the office in the building, money is harder to get each day. I am hoping that we shall be lucky and get good luck in the Irish Sweep Stake ticket so that we can go somewhere in this cockeyed world and have a decent home life without worrying about how we are going to eat and sleep. I have had three summons lately on bills for which I can not get the money to pay but what can a fellow do, its pretty hard I can tell you. You see if I pack up here at the building, I can not get no dole, and that makes it worse, because I shall not be able to get anything. It's no use thinking of going to Canada because things are a dam sight worse out there.

I agree it is hard for you to live with people that are always throwing things up at you. But it is not so easy to get money now as it was when you went away. I miss the children like hell and sometimes I wonder what ever made me allow them all to go home for.

To get £100.0.0 now is a task and people simply have not got the money to spend, hence the reason why so many people are broke and down in the gutter.

But as you know, there will come a time when we shall have money and that all the hard luck days will be forgotten, I think that we are going to be happy and lucky this time with the ticket.

Love to the family Daddy.

By April, the tenor of his next letter, still written in his own hand, is a little less conciliatory. A Mr Hutchings now enters the story as some sort of intermediary largely at Irene's behest to look out for her. Clearly Irene is suffering from lack of cash and has instructed Mr Hutchings to apply some pressure to my father. In return true or false, probably half true, Emanuel has been suffering the consequences of his hard life. Although he does not know it yet, or he thinks that it is something else, he is prone to nephritis and it drags him down through the myriad of symptoms associated with the illness. In particular, Emanuel is prone to leg problems including oedema, the swelling in the leg that may result from kidney problems. He vents his frustration by reminding Irene what he has done for her. He writes:

Prudential Buildings
Plymouth

April 9th 1934

Dear Irene and Family,

Your two letters came yesterday and found me in bed, again I have had a time of it. Went to bed March 17th got up today for the first time, and now only out for a couple of hours. I have had Dr Blades here every day. Swelling in the legs and back so you see your letter about writing to Hutchings was cheerful news. But I'd... if you write to him every day of the week; I am waiting for him to come out and say anything to me. He better mind his own affairs, Police are for interfering with family troubles. Those alone are all I can do to make ends meet when sickness gets hold of anyone then everything stops.

I done everything I could to get the money to let you go over there and I find it dam hard to get money to bring you back. You wanted to go home to your mother and it was your desire to take all the kids with you. If you remember, I wanted you to leave Jenny or one of the boys, but you wanted it your own way. You see you can not have your own way all the time. When the children left me at Southampton, it nearly broke my heart but you were so cock sure that your own people were better to you than your husband.

I have done everything to get up on a better road, when I got £185.0.0 to send you away, it meant something to get that money. You wanted to go home, I sent you home. You had your way. I am paying for it now. If Mr Hutchings wants to do anything let him pay your fares back, its easy for people to talk.

I will do what I can for you and the children. But when I am not earning nothing I can not send nothing.

Tell the children as soon as I get better I will write them each a letter but I am too weak now but I thought I would drop you a line to let you know I am still alive.

Love to family Daddy

In September 1934, now recovered from his earlier ailment and seemingly prosperous, he had heard previously from Irene that Ronald has been admitted to hospital seriously ill with blood poisoning, although the true extent of the illness has yet to surface. The letter is formal and matter of fact with little joy for either reader or writer. Behind Irene's letters is the realisation that the welcome back home that she expected from her family in Canada never materialised. On the contrary, she was shunned and had to place the three children in an orphanage during her confinement until after baby Ronald was born. These were desperate times for her. She may have heard from intermediary Hutchings that far from his business failing, Emanuel's practice was doing well, or at least earning. Whatever, she had clearly made overtures to Emanuel to return to England. Emanuel, on the other hand, now well ensconced with my mother in Victoria Villas and free from paying rent for Treville Street was having nothing of it. He did not want to lose his newly found freedom. As if to verify his relative prosperity, he now has a typewriter and has clearly mastered the basic skills of layout and typing, there being very few typo amendments in his letter. He types:

Prudential Buildings
Plymouth
September 28th 1934

Dear Irene,

I received your letter today and note your remarks regarding Gordon bad head etc.

Also about you writing letters over here to those that you think that are responsible for me not writing you but I think that you have done enough damage when you wrote Mr Hutchings regarding my letter writing etc.

I am sorry that I have not been able to send you any money there before but things have not been brisk with me here and that having had a long spell sick I could not do it. I note that you say that you are applying to the immigration officer to send you back to England, well of course I can not stop you from coming over here that is if they want to assume the expense in doing so but I cannot bring myself to agree that

I would ever take up married life again, I am satisfied to live as I have been living for the past two years, regarding the children I am willing to enter into some form of agreement to provide for them, as you will see I am sending two pounds £2.0.0 this week and I intend to send one pound each week as long as this arrangement is satisfactory to you and myself. I cannot see anything good can be accomplished by we two going back and living together again, we did not agree before we left Canada and when we got here it appeared that I was always mean and cruel to you. Under the circumstances I have realised that it is best that you live your life and that I will live mine alone, I think that you are better off in your own country, I do not wish to return to Canada therefore I can assure you that I do not beg you to return to England. The children can chose for themselves where they want to go, if we can come to an arrangement about the children I will meet you half way if it is at all reasonable. Please let me know what arrangements you require or you may have a solicitor in your town to draw up a deed of separation and send it over here for my perusal. If business picks up I will make the payments larger so that you will have protection for the children.

No doubt you will agree that it is better for us to settle the matter in this manner than to be fighting all the time.

I am convinced that married life is no good and that it is not worth the candle therefore I am satisfied to remain in the atmosphere I am at present and live the life of a single man without subject to the demands of married life of staying around the house.

I trust that the Children are well and that Gordon is better, regarding the clothes promised, I shall be attending to the matter in the course of a few days.

All the best

(Signed) Emanuel Mitchell

Within three weeks the problems with baby Ronald have now been established. Irene has written and Emanuel replies on October 17th, this time in a more loving and conciliatory way emphasising his responsibility as a father and suggesting that he can help financially.

At the top of his typed letter, on the left hand side, he wrote in manuscript, 'I have sent you £2-0-0 instead of £1-0-0 no doubt you can use it' which bears out that he may have had access to more money than he was letting on either to Irene or Hutchings. He also wants Irene to keep him informed by telegraph, reinforcing that he will pick up the tab for any expenses. This is perhaps an insight into a loving father or at least one who could not bear his child to suffer. He signs himself Daddy with innumerable X's to represent kisses; a far cry from his letter of three weeks earlier.

The Prudential Buildings
Suite 4/5
Plymouth

October 17th 1934

Dear Irene,

I have written the childrens hospital this date, and have asked the superintendent to forward to me a report on the condition of Gordon.

I have also instructed that I will be responsible for the payments for the care and attendance thereto, so you have no need to worry about that item.

Your letter I received today although I can not agree with you entirely perhaps as you say its best that we do not discuss it any further.

Regarding the payments I am trying to send you something each week, in this letter I am enclosing another pound and will do so each week and a little more if possible.

Business is not any too brisk and money is hard to find but as long as I can earn it you will have some and I think you will agree one cannot do better.

I shall be writing Gordon today or first thing in the morning so he will get it in about ten days. I understand that he is out of danger, but there is nothing to stop you to send a wire to me collect this end, the post office telephone authorities will see that I get it this end, so please do not fail to wire me at once if there is anything that I should know urgently.

I will notify the telephone people here that you may wire at my expense pay at this end on receipt of the wire. A night letter costs four shillings and twopence, so you will know what to do in the future, I don't want you to spend any of the money I send you for wires, I think that if you take this letter to the local telegraph office they will allow you to wire me with this understanding.

My telephone number in Plymouth is 3591, and your wires are always charged to me through the quarterly accounts from Exeter in other words when I wire you I simply phone the message to the telegraph department of the post office and then I get the bill quarter day.

The bill says something about an operation, but as you know I have little information at hand concerning Gordon's illness all I know is that he was suffering from blood poisoning.

I hope the children are alright and that Gordon will soon be well again, I should like to know when he leaves the hospital and the name of the medical practitioner in attendance.

As I told you in the last letter, the insurance policies are still being paid by me and think that you all the policy's with you, but you have nothing to worry about in that instance.

Hoping that you received the last money alright, and that this reaches you safe.

All the best to you and the children

xxxxDaddyxxxxxx

The next available letter and the last of the collection found in America is dated some six months later, again typed, but with many more typos which suggests that he may have been hurrying or wrestling with his conscience. Irene had clearly been candid in her correspondence with Mr Hutchings. In turn, Emanuel had to deal with the sometimes over informed intermediary. Once more the subject of reconciliation had been raised in earlier letters of the year and Emanuel continued his stance of apportioning as much blame on Irene. He refers to the car journey taking Irene and the children to Southampton docks where Irene refers to it being "the last time I shall see you". Emanuel clearly does not want to return to Canada and if Irene returns to England, Emanuel will not pay, nor live with her as husband and wife, rather suggesting the children be distributed between them. He encloses money to soften the blow. Once more he signs himself Daddy with numerous kisses.

Prudential Buildings
Suite 4/5
Plymouth

April 18th 35

Dear Irene,

    I have seen the letter or the letter was read to me by Hutchings in which you state many things about me some of it I must say that it was quite unkind and there was no need to mention in your letter to Hutchings what he already knew. I must say that you pick one of the greatest enemies when you wrote to him, he would no doubt show this letter to any person whom may have any faith in my ability. But however we will not quarrel about writing to Hutchings or his wife or anyone else for that part. You wanted to go home and if you refresh your memory, how many times have I heard you wish you were out of the country and with your people. Did you not say when driving up to Southampton, I suppose this will be the last time I shall see you, many times too numerous to state you have thrown nasty things up which was better left unsaid, however the money was borrowed for you to go home and after great efforts you were sent to Halifax N.S. in good clothes likewise the children. I do not want to escape the obligations of my family, I am willing to have Gordon and Jennie over here will pay their passage and educate them, David no doubt would sooner stay over there with you therefore I have no objections in that instant. I am also willing to pay you £1 per week providing you get in touch with a reputable solicitor at Halifax and sign the agreement that was sent you.

    Do you think that it is best that you see a solicitor in your town and have him write me so that we can get the matter settled decently, writing letters to Hutchings will not settle any dispute all he can do is make use of them to his friends against me. But if you want to write to him do so by all means I don't care he is not my friend and I do not remember when he was a friend of yours. People that travel in sheeps clothing needs watching but often they get bitten by the wolf.

Well I am sending you two pounds (£2.0.0.) Let me know about Jennie and Gordon, they are both old enough to say where they want to live, besides I know Canada and I know what can of a deal they gave me and I would not like my son or daughter to have the same brand of justice that was shewn me when I was in your country. I doubt that you will agree that both of the kids would like to see their father even tho you may be so angry as to turn them against me. I hope that your mother and father are well the insurances for the children and your parents are still being paid by me. I do not have the policies as I find that they are not around here.

All the best and by the way if the children ask you did not get your xmas present it was not my fault. It was sent early enough and it was not returned to me.

I would like to hear further about the parcel, as your letter to Hutchings did not speak any to well about me not sending a card.

Love to the family
Daddyxxxxxxxxxxxx

Irene never again saw Emanuel and Emanuel never again saw his children by her.

****

For some time, Emanuel had been hobnobbing with the great and good of the Plymouth business set, looking for opportunities to expand his enterprise (or get himself out of his present jam). Osteopathy in England was becoming increasingly popular as a recognised treatment. So much so that Emanuel said to those interested that a new Bill would shortly be placed before Parliament allowing practitioners greater freedom. Emanuel was alive with anticipation. If this Bill were to be passed, he wanted to be in the vanguard to become a leading figure in the West of England. The workhouse boy had arrived at the zenith of his influence. He was now talking on level terms with local venture capitalists, looking for a new property to be his centre of osteopathic excellence. What's more, he was confident, convincing and being taken seriously. An underlying theme could have been that given the severity of the depression and perhaps dwindling business in Plymouth, it might be a better option to borrow money, to try and cash-in on his speciality by having his own residential centre. An over view today would see this as an incredibly risky gamble. Since most people save their money during such periods of economic gloom, now as then, I suspect the omens were not very good.

The backer for my father's next project was a local Plymouth businessman called Mr Daw. He was a landowner whose interests extended to the dormitory villages edging Dartmoor, fast becoming popular for Plymouth gentry. Yelverton, just fifteen minutes drive from Plymouth, was extremely gentrified with lavish hotels and Home County style housing for those in the professions. Just a little further on from Yelverton, on the road to Princetown and the infamous Dartmoor prison, was the small, sheltered hamlet of Dousland. It had its own railway station and close by, on the opposite side of the road stood a large double fronted Edwardian mansion. The house was up for sale; it was called Alexandra Villas. Emanuel salivated at the prospect; it was just what he was looking for. The deal was done. My mother put up the deposit and Mr Daw the principal sum.

Twenty-one years before, when Emanuel left Holsworthy for Plymouth to join the Navy, the train halted at Tavistock waiting for the London train. As he surveyed the station from the train window he recalled seeing a fingerboard on the other platform, which detailed, 'Via Yelverton for Dousland, Burrator and Princetown.' At the time he had wondered what a Dous was or might have been. Perhaps he would now find out? The elements were now in place for the next step in my father's life and another adventure.

****

Notes

The twenty thousand ton ship, Duchess of York, served the Canadian Pacific line and was mobilised for war in 1940 as a troop transport. It served with great distinction. In 1943 it was sunk off Morocco during the North African Landings associated with Operation Torch. RMS Ascania served throughout WW2 as an armed merchant cruiser before returning briefly for civilian passenger use. She again saw service during the Suez campaign before being broken up in 1957. The railway line from Plymouth closed in the 1960's along with the track to Princetown via Yelverton and Dousland. They are now walkways of great beauty. Plymouth was severely bombed during WW2 and Treville Street and the Prudential Building on Bedford Road were wholly destroyed. Plymouth was completely rebuilt after WW2 with many buildings faced in a light coloured Portland stone. Apart from one or two landmarks, my father would not recognise the city at all; such was the level of destruction. If he had been living in either location during WW2 the chances are that he and my mother would have perished in the bombing.

Chapter 8

The Beginning of the End

The years 1933 and 1934 were not particularly eventful for Prime Minister Ramsey McDonald's Labour Government, although the UK did see trade union membership rise to four point four million. Economically, the country was still reeling from a financial depression set off by the 1929 stock market crash and was struggling to get back on its feet. In 1932, the nation saw the Jarrow March. A vast army of the unemployed from the North East of England made its way to London on foot and confronted Parliament, demanding the means to earn and feed their children. These were not good times. The English social climate was one of weariness, unemployment and a lack of confidence in the future.

What now confronted Emanuel was a far cry from those heady, Edwardian days when he first set off on his adventures. The Empire was still there, but the national coffers had been exhausted in a catastrophic world war and the following economic slump. This was hardly the time to contemplate bold commercial ventures. In Germany, on the other hand, the Nazis had come to power the same year. Hitler became Chancellor and supposedly, a Dutch communist promptly burnt down the Reichstag parliamentary building ending all democratic government in Germany. Far from a depression, the dynamics inside Germany were breathtaking as Britain and America stumbled and then fell into confusion and disharmony. During this time, Emanuel began a brief flirtation with Oswald Mosley's blackshirts, a far right wing fascist group, although his enthusiasm soon faded.

In America, the year saw the unemployed population rise to a staggering thirteen million. The man my father heard about in 1914 and who opened the Cabrillo Bridge at San Diego nineteen years before, had now begun his first administration as President Roosevelt.

Later in 1933 there would be an attempt on his life. FDR, as he became known had promised the American people a "new deal". It would take four consecutive administrations to bring this deal to fulfilment, but he did it. On a brighter, more optimistic note, in late 1933 the foundations for the Golden Gate Bridge were laid in San Francisco. Closer to home and in the bleak, British, political and economic climate of the time, Emanuel Mitchell and Lenora Congdon were to embark on a huge, optimistic, ultimately risky financial gamble.

My mother and father completed the purchase of Alexandra Villas, Dousland. The agreed price complete with basic furnishings was £3,200, a hefty sum in those days. My mother had provided the deposit of £500 and Mr Daw the necessary investment of £2,700. As if to confirm that this was the beginning of a new chapter in their lives, the house name Alexandra Villas was changed to Dream Tor. In their naivety they saw this venture as the culmination of their aspirations. The purchase of Dream Tor was completed just six months or so after the Plymouth court case.

This impressive 24 bedroom mansion was constructed on three floors with attics in the steep, dark grey Cornish slate roof. The plain cement rendered exterior was embellished by balconies on the first and second floors with balustrades of turned wooden spindles under a white painted handrail. Large, quartered sash windows were evenly spaced on all the floors giving the whole building the necessary symmetry. It was a prestigious, impressive building, with a certain Home Counties, gentrified look that was all the rage at the turn of the century. Several other buildings in the area mimicked this particular style including the more impressive Devon Tors Hotel at Yelverton. The array of chimneys had been cleverly arranged in the centre of the building so each half of the house mirrored the other. The original intention had been to have two separate houses. Finally, the house was situated more or less on the road front with a stream, or Dartmoor leat as it is called locally, running in front. Behind the mansion was a large lozenge shaped garden and a row of 4 stables and two carriage houses. At the bottom of the hundred metres garden on a separate plot, was a further Edwardian private house constructed in the same style, but on a smaller scale.

Dream Tor (Railway line and station to the right)

How easy it would be for clients to arrive by train from Plymouth just twenty minutes away, Emanuel observed. In the accessible countryside he hoped to set up the first osteopathic centre in the West Country catering for the well to do. Here he would provide "the cure". At least, that was the general idea he had earlier explained to others to secure the loan. If it were ever to look the part, the conversion of Alexandra Villas into Dream Tor was a huge undertaking. It would involve the need to employ staff and obtain numerous items of expensive equipment and extra furniture. It was inevitable that there would be a number of creditors. Once more, fate was to take a hand in my father's affairs.

The Osteopathy Bill that Emanuel hoped would be passed by Parliament disappeared off the statute book, if it was ever there at all. Within a short period Lenora and Emanuel were left with a huge, probably unsaleable property and little or no business. Yelverton and Dousland were more than well served by quality hotels, all of which were struggling to survive in depressed times. In addition, Emanuel had to pay a mortgage and the upkeep of the premises, along with the normal utility and county tax bills. The economic climate, let alone medical legislation, was not there to encourage the type of investment and development that Emanuel envisaged. Very quickly, the reality of their situation confronted them.

In late 1934, in an effort to extricate themselves from their situation, plan B was to turn the facilities into a nursing or rest home. Certainly, when Kelly's Business Directory for the years 1935/36/37/38 was published, both the osteopathic practice at Prudential Buildings and Dream Tor were listed in Emanuel's name along with an accommodation address at Victoria Villas, mother's marital home. Plan B was still not enough to make ends meet. The next idea was to turn Dream Tor into a Country Club, whilst still reserving some of the bedrooms for nursing requirements. The anecdotal evidence is that the Country Club became a partial success, particularly at weekends when Plymothians would come out to the country for light dining, dancing and relaxing at the bar. Thelma talks of these being happy, if short lived times. It was, of course, a feast and famine situation. The summer months brought in the numbers and good profit at weekends. During weekdays and the long winter months, however, there was only Emanuel's income from his practice at Prudential Buildings to pay the bills. At the same time, my mother's savings began to dwindle alarmingly.

Emanuel kept his practice running in Plymouth whilst my mother became Dream Tor's manageress or housekeeper. The arrangement was sustainable providing Emanuel's practice provided a good income. It didn't. The custom for his practice began to drop off and likewise the country club and the nursing home business at Dream Tor. There had been no patient problems, quite the contrary, but the economic climate was just not there for people to spend their money on what might have been viewed as the frivolous activities associated with fringe medicine. By the end of 1935, business was so bad that Dream Tor had to be shut up for the whole of the winter of 1935/36, whilst Emanuel and Lenora retreated to Victoria Villas. Once more Emanuel's survival instinct took over and he crossed the boundaries of accepted practice and behaviour. To increase the room usage at Dream

Tor and to encourage clients, he had allowed unaccompanied ladies to be available, offering their services, discreetly of course, to gentlemen. But even this was not enough, or perhaps just too risky.

Dream Tor ran on for another year by the skin of its teeth until the winter of 1936/37. Servicing the loan from Mr Daw and paying the routine bills and wages had been difficult. Around this time the story takes on a macabre side. The gossip was that my father was in some way involved in carrying out pregnancy terminations. It was said that unfortunate girlfriends of Naval Officers who had found themselves pregnant, could receive a termination from Mr Mitchell who had been a Doctor in the United States. As the summer season for 1936 ended and Dream Tor was prepared for closure during the winter months, it was fairly obvious that something needed to be done. The collective income was not sufficient to pay the outgoings on the three properties: Dream Tor, Prudential Buildings and finally Victoria Villas. The symptoms of this decline during 1936 show in delayed payment of bills and the frequency of minor court summonses for unpaid accounts. The truth about what happened next may never be known, but the consequences for my father and mother were profound and were to haunt them for the rest of their lives.

Late into the night of Sunday, January 24th and the early morning of Monday, January 25th, 1937, in heavy rain, catastrophe struck. Fire erupted at Dream Tor. Witnesses saw sparks flying from five miles away, so the local newspapers later reported. Gradually, throughout the night the fire gathered momentum, quickly becoming a minor inferno. The fire brigade vehicles from both Yelverton and Tavistock attended and the ferocity of the fire was such that water had to be pumped from the leat (stream) to quell the flames. Locals, who were awoken by the kerfuffle, heard the panic-stricken whinnying of horses in the stables. Emanuel had let these out for livery to raise extra cash. Thanks to the brave act of Mr Coussens, a local stable lad, the horses were saved and released into a nearby paddock. Meanwhile the ferocity of the fire was such that water had to be sprayed onto nearby houses to protect them from the raging inferno. Reports said that the fire spread from its origins in the top half of the building and then spread laterally causing the majority of the building to collapse, leaving only the centre set of chimneys standing and the balustrading hanging precariously, "Mercifully the building was unoccupied," said Fire Captain H Kitto, adding, "We are lucky that the flames did not spread to adjoining buildings."

There was nothing to be salvaged other than a radiogram rescued by an onlooker who was able to extract it from the main hall before the fire had spread. Curiously, there was little furniture to be seen broken, burnt or otherwise in the rubble that remained. Collapsed brickwork joists and charred wood lay all around the smoking ruins in the dawn light, with hoses criss-crossing the road from the leat. A hurdle (piece of lattice fence) had been placed over the leat supported by rocks to dam it, thus causing a pool upstream, from which water could be pumped to replenish the fire tenders. As the morning light welcomed the new day, policemen arrived from Plymouth to stand guard around the ruins. The onlookers were not quite sure if this was to prevent pillaging, or to conserve evidence of what seemed a mighty curious outbreak of fire on such a cold, rainy and windy evening.

From that moment on, rumour and counter rumour were rife. When I returned to the scene of the fire seventy years later and spoke to locals, that same rumour was still rife about the 'Great Fire of Dousland'. There had been nothing before and nothing since on such a scale in the area. Those who worked casually at Dream Tor were well aware of the ever reducing circumstances and the intimate details of the goings on. It was inevitable that gossip would eventually get around the Burrator Inn and Meavy Oak village pubs. Like all apocryphal stories, it would also grow in the telling to become some way from the truth. Two and two had been put together and my father had been tried in the eyes of the locals, so I was told, found guilty of arson and sent to prison. That was most certainly not the case.

The story my mother and father provided to both the police and insurers was quite plausible. There was always a need, they said, to keep the building aired and reasonably dry, particularly during the unoccupied winter months. From time to time they lit fires in various grates around the house to encourage the flow of warm, dry air. Sometimes they also erected clothes horses around a fire to air linen. It would appear, they suggested, that despite every precaution being taken, a dying ember had jumped out of the fire starting the inferno.

Mr Mitchell went on to say that he had left Dream Tor that evening after erecting a clothes horse to air laundry, before going into Plymouth to collect his "wife". (At 1 pm in the morning?)

The Burnt out Remains (Plymouth Evening Herald)

By coincidence, the Prudential Insurance Company had insured Dream Tor. In due course, the company sent out their investigator and assessor Mr Hamley, to check over the ruins and assess the damage liability on behalf of the insurer. In the meantime, the fire was well reported by the local newspapers where the Plymouth Evening Herald fanned the flames of controversy (I could not resist the pun) with the banner headline: '*Mystery of Origin of Outbreak in Unoccupied Premises*'.

In April 1937, in connection with the circumstances surrounding the fire, Emanuel once more made the headlines when he brought a prosecution against Mr Hamley (the Prudential assessor) and his friend Mr Coles. This became Emanuel's thirteenth appearance in court, but this time he held the role of prosecutor. The headlines of the Plymouth Evening Herald read *'Osteopath Accuses City Business Men. Prosecutor Asks Chairman to Retire'*. In this totally bizarre prosecution brought by my father, presumably before the outcome of the insurance claim was made known, he accuses Messrs Hamley and Cole of breaking into a garage at Dream Tor, (damage valued at seven shillings) and stealing coke, (value twelve shillings and sixpence). Emanuel's principal witness is my mother, described in the papers as, *'a mysterious lady,'* whose evidence was that she, as the Dream Tor housekeeper, did not give permission to Messrs Hamley and Cole to remove anything. Not content with that, Emanuel also suggested that the Chairman of the Bench might be biased! Not surprisingly, the case was dismissed. But something had started that neither my mother, nor Emanuel bargained for; the wholesale reporting of their lives in the newspapers.

This unwelcome press intrusion into their lives was to have grave consequences for the relationship between my mother and her father. A year before in 1936 Sidney John and Elizabeth Reep had retired to a cottage in Bridestowe village. Up to that time Lenora had remained in contact with her father and mother, albeit that Sidney John was sceptical about the relationship with Emanuel, particularly as he was a married man. Events were to change once the newspapers got hold of the Dream Tor story. As revelation after revelation was reported in the newspapers, so shame and embarrassment were heaped on to my grandparents. In Sidney John's mind, to be married and separated was one thing, but to be co-habiting with a married man, where there was innuendo about all sorts of possible criminal goings on, was simply too much. Grandfather made the decision to disown his daughter. Enough was enough; he would not talk of her again.

In this he kept to his word and when in 1947 he died, he died intestate. My grandmother, Elizabeth, would take a slightly softer view towards her only daughter and remained in contact with her clandestinely. For Thelma, life was to take on a peripatetic existence as she was shunted from one boarding school to another. She was destined to meet up with her mother only during school holidays. Like her grandparents, she was also to suffer embarrassment and humiliation, with the addition of torment from other children as newspaper articles came to the attention of her peers in a convent boarding school in Okehampton.

The site today with the back of the stable block (Rt) visible

If matters looked black that spring and summer of 1937, worse was to come. In keeping with all disasters, creditors, not unnaturally, clamoured for their bills and accounts to be settled. In consequence a series of petty prosecutions were brought against my father throughout 1937. These were largely for unpaid tax bills, suppliers' invoices and parking fines. My mother cleared the prosecutions against herself, but those prosecutions against Emanuel typically, remained unanswered. All of this was again reported in minute detail in the regional press and gloated over by the villagers of Bridestowe (my mother's home) where the locals were only too anxious to register their contempt for my mother.

But it was not all bad news. In due course the Prudential

Insurance Company paid up. My father said later in court that he received the princely sum of £1500 for Dream Tor's rebuilding cost. Contrary to all the gossip, there was no case of arson to answer. On hearing that Emanuel had received the insurance money Mr Daw and other creditors decided to act quickly. They too wanted to be paid off before the insurance payout had been expended elsewhere. Acting in unison they threatened to bring a prosecution for bankruptcy against my father if he did not pay up. Emanuel's counter argument was that if Dream Tor was to be re-built and once more produce an income to pay back his creditors, he would need to re-invest that money in rebuilding Dream Tor. There was logic in this reply, although perhaps it was naïve to believe that he would ever take that course of action. Deeds, in this instance, speak louder than words. There is no record that rebuilding estimates were ever presented.

The patience of the creditors soon ran out. If Emanuel would not pay, they would bankrupt him. Under threat of bankruptcy Emanuel became both elusive and reclusive. It seems that during the period immediately after the fire he had also closed down the osteopathic practice in Plymouth, retrieved and sold valuables and had begun a period of wandering, living in a caravan with my mother. (The caravan can just be seen in the Dream Tor picture behind the house.) During the same period the house at 18, Victoria Villas was also sold. The two of them were now cash rich with the proceeds of Victoria Villas and the Dream Tor Insurance money.

Emanuel's intention was to disappear into the English countryside hoping that the hue and cry would naturally exhaust itself. This was never going to happen. In time the court bailiffs would catch up with them at a number of different, "accommodation addresses" including a house number in a new development that had not even been built! Emanuel was stringing them along. In truth, Emanuel and Lenora knew that they needed a permanent address. In late 1937, with their property pay outs, Emanuel, Lenora and Thelma rented an up-market flat in Clifton Gardens, Maida Vale, London. Emanuel had made no attempt to attend the various petty offence hearings in the Plymouth Magistrates Court. He simply refused to declare where he was living, or had moved on by the time the Bailiffs had caught up with him. His disrespect for the law was total. By the winter of 1937/8, the creditors had no option but to apply to make my father bankrupt. To this action, sensing the possibility that he might just might, be able to bullshit his way out of trouble, my father did respond. He was now about to embark on his fourteenth appearance before the bench, but this time in a Bankruptcy Court.

The hearing before Mr Dobell, the Registrar of the Plymouth Bankruptcy Court, was due to be heard on May 6th 1938. Mr Goodman was appointed by the court to act as the Official Receiver on behalf of the Crown. Seventeen months had elapsed since the date of the fire. This had given Emanuel and Lenora plenty of time to make whatever alternative arrangements they deemed necessary to dispose of their assets and cash.

Plymouth Law Courts (Before the Blitz)

What now follows is an edited version taken from the various court transcripts of the bankruptcy hearing as reported in the daily newspapers of the time. The reader will be in the privileged position of knowing the truth from earlier chapters and can follow the proceedings as the all knowing 'fly on the wall.' Emanuel simply thought that it was a bankruptcy case and no doubt that he could bluff his way out of trouble, as before. The whole world was now to be acquainted with the tacky life of Emanuel Mitchell Esq.

But first, what Emanuel did not know and what he was entirely unprepared for was that Irene had been informed of her husband's shenanigans and double life from a friend she had made at Treville St and with whom she was in regular contact by letter. In the past as we know, she had moved heaven and earth to testify on Emanuel's behalf. Now the shoe of loyalty was on the other foot. Hell hath no fury like a woman scorned. Irene was to write to the court to provide the official Receiver with such an in-depth background on Emanuel's criminal past that any defence would seem to be a waste of time. Yet, Emanuel would not give up easily, pulling every stunt that he could.

The following note is provided to help readers understand the terminology used in English courts of law. Bankruptcy is dealt with through the specific Bankruptcy Courts which are part of the Chancery Division. The key individuals of this court are the Registrar and the Official Receiver. The Official Receiver is a civil servant, in our case Mr Goodman. He is a servant in 'The Insolvency Service' and an officer of the court. He will be notified by the court of the bankruptcy or winding-up order, which in our case had been presented by Emanuel's creditors. He will then be responsible through his staff for administering the initial stage of the insolvency case. This stage includes collecting and protecting any assets and investigating the causes of the bankruptcy or winding up. The latter is normally done through a 'Hearing in the Bankruptcy Court'. This is what is reported below, a hearing of my father's case. The Registrar is the person of the courts below the judge who will literally hear the case and ensure fair play by the law. If necessary, he can remand or adjourn the case to be heard before the judge. A Registrar will be a qualified barrister. There is no equivalent in the US courts to a barrister other than an Attorney at Law. However, as he is acting on behalf of the judiciary, the Registrar in this case may equate to the District Attorney. A solicitor is simply another name for a lawyer or attorney. For a solicitor to become a barrister and represent a defendant in court or prosecute in the court, he must first be called to the "bar".

May 6th was a very pleasant spring day with just a hint of summer in the air. The oak panelled court room was alive with a buzz of anticipation as the Registrar took his seat below the Royal Coat of Arms which hung on the wall above him. The public gallery was half full with the usual spectators associated with creditors. Having visually noted that the court was assembled the Registrar banged his gavel and called on Mr Goodman, the Official Receiver, to open… The Plymouth Evening Herald journalist flipped open his note book, licked the end of his pencil and began to write…

Plymouth Evening Herald May 6th 1938

DEBTOR NOT AT PLYMOUTH EXAMINATION

QUESTION OF APPEAL

Emanuel Frederick Mitchell, osteopath, of 16 Victoria Villas, St Budeaux, carrying on business at the Prudential Buildings, Plymouth, did not appear for public examination in the Plymouth Bankruptcy Court today. The examination was adjourned. Mr A.N.F. Goodman, Official Receiver, told the Registrar, Mr E.S. Dobell that the debtor had been served with the customary notice. However, Mr Mitchell was appealing against the receiving order. Mr Mitchell's appeal was scheduled to be heard on May 16th next. In the meantime, there had been no other communication with Mr Mitchell. The court presumed therefore, that Mr Mitchell was under the impression that he need not attend this hearing. However, Mr Goodman went on to say, this was only an assumption on his behalf. Mr Mitchell had sent Mr Goodman, the Receiver, a statement of affairs of a kind, but this had to be returned to him for amendment and completion. At the date of this hearing, Mr Goodman had not received back the completed forms. As a result, there seemed no alternative but to adjourn the case. (*Round one to Emanuel*). Mr Goodman went on to suggest that the adjournment should be subsequent to the date of the appeal. Mr W. Broad, who appeared for creditors, said in reply to the Registrar that he also had not received any communication from Mr Mitchell.

The Registrar suggested adjourning the examination for a month; but Mr Goodman disagreed, expressing a desire to deal with this case as soon as possible. The next hearing was fixed for May 20th, just two weeks ahead, and four days after the appeal that took place on May

16th.

Emanuel had won round one. His aim from now on would be to delay and procrastinate for as long as possible knowing that putting time and distance between himself and the court would allow him to secure other arrangements for himself and his money. Not surprisingly, at the next hearing his tactics remain the same.

Plymouth Evening Herald 20th May 1938

COURT "BEING TRIFLED WITH" BY PLYMOUTH OSTEOPATH SAYS OFFICIAL RECEIVER EXAMINATION IS AGAIN ADJOURNED

Emanuel Frederick Mitchell, an osteopath of 16 Victoria Villas, St Budeaux, who is carrying on a business at the Prudential Buildings, Plymouth has applied for a further adjournment of his public examination at Plymouth Bankruptcy Court. He has indicated that that he would now like to be legally represented. He asked the court to adjourn his case for thirty days. The Official Receiver, Mr A.N.F Goodman, suggested a week and the Registrar consented to an adjournment until June 3rd.

Whilst holding the Testament in his right hand Mr Mitchell said, "I wish to tell the court that I object to taking the oath, but I am prepared to take a solemn affirmation. I certainly promise to tell the truth. I must tell the Court that I was in the Master of the Rolls Court yesterday afternoon with regard to this case. I was advised that that if I wanted anything to be heard in the Higher Court, I must first bring it in the Lower Court."

COURT'S "REMINDER"

Mr Mitchell went on to say, "I am not prepared at this time because I am not represented. I wish to be represented after hearing what the Master of the Rolls said yesterday. I am going to make an application for the adjournment of my public examination for 30 days, so that I may have a representative. I now believe that it is in my best interest to be represented by a specialist lawyer from London who is an expert in Bankruptcy law and who is best qualified to handle my affairs. I certainly do not have anyone in mind from Plymouth. May I also ask the Court if Mr Goodman's right to confiscate my letters be rescinded?"

Mr Goodman took to his feet and replied, "Mr Mitchell has my full permission to inspect any letters connected with business that were in the Official Receiver possession. However, I categorically refuse to rescind the order. On Monday last you were in the Divisional Court. They dismissed your appeal against the receiving order made by the Registrar. You asked for leave of appeal to the Court of Appeal and it was refused."

Unruffled Mr Mitchell replied. "That is correct. Then, I made application before the Master of the Rolls yesterday afternoon and raised that question. Now I am asking that I be protected from now on and represented by a qualified solicitor. The Court has reminded me that I have made a mistake."

Mr Goodman was clearly irritated by Mr Mitchell's late request for representation.
"I object to this altogether. It seems to me that the Court is being trifled with. For some reason or other this debtor is very anxious, as far as I can see, to avoid the investigation of his affairs by the Court," he stated testily. "When the receiving order was made by Mr Dobell, the Registrar, Mr Mitchell did not, in any way, apply for a stay of proceedings. Come to it, he has not even now filed a statement of his affairs! All he has done has been to send me some sort of document which had to be returned to him for correction. He gave the address of the Royal Hotel, Woburn Street, Russell Square, London. Let me tell the court that all the papers addressed by me to that hotel have been returned. I do not want to prejudice the man in any shape or form, but in the first place I want an address where he can be found."

Once more, contritely, Mr Mitchell replied, "My address in London is Claygate Road, Hinchley Wood, Surrey. Letters will reach me at that address."

"Do you undertake to notify the Court of any change of address?" asked Mr Dobell.

"I promise to do so," said Mr Mitchell, "and I pledge to send a statement of affairs to the court." In mitigation my father continued, "I regret that I did not receive your earlier communications from the Official Receiver requesting the corrected information."

Mr Dobell now wished to conclude the hearing. "I am prepared to allow an adjournment on condition that Mr Mitchell notifies the court of any change of address and completes the statement of affairs that I previously requested."

In reply, Mr Mitchell replied that he promised to do so.

In closing the proceedings Mr Dobell looking directly at Mr Mitchell said with some emphasis. "Mr Mitchell, you must attend to be examined at the next hearing regardless of your solicitor being present or not."

It was again round two to Emanuel. How could the court contact him on Claygate Road if he did not give a number? He had won a further stay of execution waffling his way through court, but now seriously underestimating its intelligence. He may have thought that he was laughing at the court, but slowly by slowly his true character was being revealed. He could not hoodwink the court for much longer.

Plymouth Evening Herald 3rd June 1938

WEALTHY MYSTERY WOMAN'S LOANS TO PLYMOUTH OSTEOPATH: AMAZING STORY MAN WHO OWNED COUNTRY CLUB ADMITS CONVICTIONS. TELLS HOW HE WENT TO UNDERTAKERS' PARLOURS AND STUDIED THE BODIES.

Emanuel Frederick Mitchell, an osteopath, appeared at Plymouth Bankruptcy Court today for the adjourned hearing into his financial affairs. Responding to the Official Receiver, Mr A.N.F. Goodman, the debtor said that at the time of the receiving order he was carrying on business at the Prudential Buildings, Plymouth, as an osteopath. In connection with his statement of affairs, liabilities were estimated at £767, with assets valued at 7s. 3d. The assets had been absorbed in preferential claims. (Assessing the value of his assets, he had clearly disposed of many of them already).

Following the introduction, Mr Goodman opened the proceedings addressing Mr Mitchell, the debtor.

"At the preliminary examination you told me that you were 41 years of age and went to America in 1913 and served in the Canadian Army until 1915?"

Mr Mitchell replied, "It was a little later than that."

Mr Goodman continued, "You stated that you then returned to Canada and obtained various situations, chiefly of a nursing nature, and that you studied osteopathy, obtained a doctor's degree and then commenced to practise?"

"Yes, that is correct." Mr Mitchell confirmed.

"You returned to England in 1930 Mr Mitchell?"

"Yes, that is correct."

Now rising to the drama of the occasion, Mr Goodman looked Mitchell straight in the eye. "Is it a fact that you were deported from Canada Mr Mitchell?"

Mr Mitchell was momentarily caught unaware and replied defensively, "No, I was repatriated."

Mr Goodman was now aware that he had Mr Mitchell on the back foot.
"Did you, while in Canada or America, adopt various names?"

"I do not think so," Mr Mitchell replied apprehensively.

"Were you known in America as, James E. Smith, L. L. Moody, Edward Mitchell, O.P. Johnson, Charles B. Collins, George Thomas and Emanuel Frederick Childs?" Mr Goodman demanded.

Clearing his throat, Mr Mitchell replied. "I did use the names Thomas and Childs, but I never, ever used the other names."

The pace of Mr Goodman's questions accelerated. "Were you prosecuted in San Diego, in 1916, under the name of Childs, for using or uttering fictitious cheques?"

"I cannot remember that," replied Mr Mitchell defensively.

"Come, come Mr Mitchell, Were you or were you not prosecuted in San Diego in 1916?" Mr Goodman repeated now slightly agitated.

"I am not in a position to say," Mr Mitchell replied.

By now exasperation was beginning to show in Mr Goodman's questioning. "You are not going to ask this Court to believe that you cannot remember whether it was a fact?"

"I do not remember," Mr Mitchell replied once more clearing his throat.

To the unknowing, the revelations were now coming thick and fast. My father had no inkling that so much of his prior history had been discovered. He was momentarily distracted by how this could be. But a woman scorned...

"Were you prosecuted or incarcerated in San Quentin Prison in 1916 in the name of Childs?" continued Mr Goodman.

"I do not remember that," Mr Mitchell replied. "Any prosecutions that I may have had in the United States were of a political character."

"Were you again prosecuted in Los Angeles in 1925 in the name of Mitchell for violation of the medical law?" Mr Goodman continued.

"Yes, I was prosecuted under the violation of the Medical Practice Act." Mr. Mitchell replied, adding, "I was one of those working to establish osteopathy."

The Receiver was clearly now on a roll, and realised the debtor's uneasiness. "Were you also prosecuted in Los Angeles in 1926 for attempted extortion?" Mr Goodman continued confidently.

"That was not the charge. It was a political charge. I was at that time attached to a political party." Mr Mitchell replied tersely.

"Were you also prosecuted and convicted in 1926 in Los Angeles for petty larceny?"

"No, not to my knowledge," Mr Mitchell replied.

"Were you prosecuted for forgery in Los Angeles in 1926?"

"I do not remember that." Mr Mitchell answered, now clearly unnerved.

"The information at my disposal is that you were prosecuted or convicted on five counts of forgery." Mr Goodman declared.

"No, if my memory serves me right, I was attached to a party… a number of us were indicted for forgery of documents. The charge was reduced to aiding and abetting," Mr Mitchell responded, starting to panic somewhat.

"Were you convicted of forgery in 1927 at Los Angeles and put on five years probation?"

"I agree… but that was a political offence." Mr Mitchell replied, his manner suggesting that this was surely a trifling matter.

"Forgery hardly seems a political offence." maintained Mr Goodman.

"I was bound over for five years," confessed Mr Mitchell.

"Is it a fact that you violated your probation?" Mr Goodman continued.

"I took the advice of my attorney, who told me that the best thing I could do was to leave the country," Mr Mitchell intoned, exhaustion now beginning to show on his face.

"Were you prosecuted in 1929 in Vancouver in the name of Emanuel Mitchell for obtaining money by false pretence?" quizzed Mr Goodman, now relishing the moment and Mitchell's discomfort.

"No. It arose out of the Medical Practice Act in the Province of British Columbia," asserted Mr Mitchell.

"There is apparently another prosecution against you in 1929, at Oakalla" Mr Goodman announced.

"That was the same thing. Osteopaths could be thrown into gaol very easily," Mr Mitchell explained.

"Was that in the name of George Thomas? The records would show that. Were you sentenced to six months imprisonment?" Mr Goodman read from a note.

"Yes," Mr Mitchell replied.

"By that time, apparently, you had decided to leave Canada, or the authorities had come to the conclusion that they preferred your absence to your presence," suggested Mr Goodman.

"That is incorrect, Mr Goodman." Mr Mitchell replied, now visibly fatigued.

"I have to put it to you that you were deported." Mr Goodman stated.

"I was not... I served in the Canadian Expeditionary Force. I signed an agreement. I was repatriated to England, and was treated so when landing from the ship Duchess of York." Mr Mitchell answered.

"That was in 1929?"

"Yes." Mr Mitchell confirmed.

"At that time you were accompanied by your wife and three children." Mr Goodman stated.

"Yes." Mr Mitchell confirmed.

"Did you enter a public institution at Southampton?" Mr Goodman continued.

"Yes, I was forced to, as my money had been taken up with counsel's fees," Mr Mitchell answered.

"What happened to your wife?" Mr Goodman questioned.

"She went back to Canada." Mr Mitchell answered abruptly.

"Are you supporting her?" Mr Goodman enquired.

"No," came the clipped response from Mr Mitchell.

"Do you know how she is living?" Mr Goodman continued.

"No… there has been no correspondence." Mr Mitchell answered.

"On your return to England, you worked for a railway company?" queried Mr Goodman.

"Yes." Mr Mitchell confirmed.

"That hardly seems consistent with medical work?" queried Mr Goodman.

"When I landed here I was broke. I came to Plymouth and afterwards went to Holsworthy, the place of my birth. Through the kindness of an inspector on the railway I obtained a position, pick and shovel work." Mr Mitchell explained.

Mr Goodman then asked Mr Mitchell questions concerning various degrees obtained in America.

"Did you get them at a University?"

"No. They were osteopathic degrees and not medical degrees." Mr Mitchell agreed.

The cross examination continued with enquiries into Mr Mitchell's training and qualifications. He was asked by Mr Goodman if he had studied dissection.

2,400 HOURS OF STUDY
Man's Story of How He Learned Dissection at Los Angeles

Mr Mitchell was now feeling more relaxed in talking about his chosen profession. "Yes, I have indeed studied dissection. This was one of the necessary studies required to qualify as an osteopath. I undertook this study for 2400 hours. I went to seven undertakers' parlours in Los Angeles, where I got my dissection study experience. It is a law of California that a student shall have so many hours of such study. I went to the parlours and studied the bodies which were being embalmed."

Now returning to the matter in hand, Mr Mitchell was asked by Mr Goodman about Dream Tor and his businesses. Mr Mitchell then described how he had first started in business as an osteopath. In the first instance, it was in Plymouth where he had premises in Treville Street. He admitted borrowing £200 from a Mrs Congdon to set up the practice. However, this money had been later repaid in full.

"Were you able to make a living as an osteopath Mr Mitchell?" continued Mr Goodman.

"Yes." Mr Mitchell responded.

"Until apparently you were prosecuted by the Medical Defence Union in 1933?" continued Mr Goodman with some degree of relish.

"Yes." Mr Mitchell confirmed.

"You were fined £10 on two charges of unlawfully using the title of surgeon and physician?" Mr Goodman enquired.

"Yes." came the curt reply from Mr Mitchell, as if hurt by this assertion that he was not qualified.

LOAN REPAID

Now leaving personal matters, Mr Goodman moved on to question Mr Mitchell about the purchase of a house known as Dream Tor at Dousland, which the debtor stated that he had purchased in 1934 for the sum of £3,200. (around £300,000 in today's money). Mr Goodman now sought to establish how the purchase was financed.
"Did you obtain £2,700 from one loan and £500 from another?" he asked.

"Yes, that is true." Mr Mitchell confirmed.

"Has the £500 been repaid?" Mr Goodman asked.

"Yes, long ago," Mr Mitchell retorted.

"Now, from what source was that £500 repaid?" Mr Goodman pressed.

"My earnings." Mr Mitchell replied and then went on to describe the business and financial climate surrounding the purchase. "I purchased Dream Tor because I felt sure that the Osteopath Bill would soon be passed in Parliament which would offer osteopaths far more opportunities in the treatment of the sick. I wanted to have the first building of its type in the West of England. But as you know, the Bill was never passed through Parliament. This was a major disappointment to me. Nevertheless, the house was partially furnished when I bought it. I had to do something, for obvious reasons, so I decided to run the premises as a Guest House. In that connection I formed the Dousland Country Club which was run by a committee, in charge of the day-to-day business."

"That's very interesting," Mr Goodman observed, "Perhaps you can tell the court who comprised the committee?"

"I am sorry, but I cannot do that. But there are records that confirm this." advised Mr Mitchell.

Once more, Mr Goodman pressed Mr Mitchell for the names of the committee members, "Now Mr Mitchell, surely you can remember the names of those who made up your committee, the organisation that oversaw your property, which set the rules. If not all of them, perhaps you can remember some of them, or one of them?"

"No I am sorry, the names have escaped me." Mr Mitchell replied. "I am sorry but my health has not been all it might these past few months. With all that has happened my mind has been in terrible turmoil."

Unmoved by this excuse, Mr Goodman continued.
"Is there a minute book recording the business Mr Mitchell?"

"Yes, but unfortunately it was destroyed in the fire," Mr Mitchell answered hoping to end the matter.

"How very convenient that the fire occurred in January, 1937." Mr Goodman said sarcastically.

"Yes." Mr Mitchell acknowledged.

"And how much insurance money did you obtain Mr Mitchell?"

"I received a cheque for £1,500. I then passed over the cheque to Mrs Congdon to whom I was financially indebted."

"And how much money had Mrs Congdon loaned you, Mr Mitchell?"

"About £1,500 or more,"

"Who is Mrs Congdon?" Mr Goodman asked expecting a full answer or description.

"I think she is a lady of means." Mr Mitchell replied, without offering further detail.

Un-ruffled Mr Goodman asked, "Is she living with her husband?"

Clearly, Mr Goodman now wished to establish what exactly the relationship was with Mrs Congdon. Mr Mitchell said that she was not living with her husband and when asked by Mr Goodman what her husband did, Mr Mitchell said at first that he did not know, but later described him as a civil servant. Mr Mitchell then went on to describe how Mrs Congdon had advanced him the money in cash to purchase Dream Tor.

Mr Goodman was surprised by this and asked Mr Mitchell "Did she never give you a cheque?"

"Yes… sometimes,"

"How many cheques did she give you, Mr Mitchell?"

"I cannot remember," Mr Mitchell replied in a subdued manner, realising that he was now in trouble with his explanation.

Rising to the occasion once more, Mr Goodman inclined his head towards the court. "Is the Court to understand that the major part of this money was advanced in cash?"

"Yes." came the reply and with that came the realisation that Mr Mitchell had fallen into a trap.

PROPERTY FROM FATHER?

"Now Mr Mitchell," Mr Goodman proposed, "I put it to you that all the money Mrs Congdon possessed was in the form of a little property that came to her from her father."

"I know nothing about that," Mr Mitchell lied.

Mr Mitchell had for some time given his address publicly as Mrs

Congdon's address at 16 Victoria Villas and since they were co-habiting it would have been most unlikely that he, who was already financially linked to her, would not have known her financial circumstances. Mr Goodman knew this was a deduction of simple logic and one that a court was unlikely to overlook.

"You are not going to convince me or the Court that you are so entirely ignorant of the financial affairs of Mrs Congdon as you would have us believe, Mr Mitchell."

"I cannot tell you how much money she had." Mr Mitchell retorted.

The sting now arrived.

Looking directly at Mr Mitchell, Mr Goodman again proposed, "I suggest to you that the handing over of this £1,500 cheque to her was simply to keep it out of the hands of the bankers and possibly the creditors."

"No! That's not so," Mr Mitchell replied, clearly now flustered, "she offered to pay the creditors in full".

"All right then, where is Mrs Congdon?" Mr Goodman demanded.

Mr Mitchell replied that he did not know (which was of course inconceivable given the situation and the known relationship between Mr Mitchell and Mrs Congdon.) Mr Goodman continued to press for an answer as Mr Mitchell felt and looked more and more uncomfortable. Finally, Mr Mitchell relaxed and addressed Mr Goodman. The hearing took another one of those bizarre, Mitchellesque twists.

"Do you want me to tell you the truth? She told me she would not come back because you, Mr Goodman, threatened to put her into prison."

Unmoved by this plea for emotional sympathy from the court, Mr Goodman spoke vehemently.

"I put it to you, Mr Mitchell, that Mrs Congdon is keeping out of the way in collusion with you."

"No!" Mr Mitchell responded. "But she is prepared to accept an apology from you."

Mr Goodman now softened his tone and stance. He spoke softly. "Mrs Congdon is never likely to get an apology from me for something which never happened. Now Mr Mitchell, let me be very clear. I and this court want to know Mrs Congdon's address."

In a gesture of selflessness or plain stupidity, Mr Mitchell replied, "I am sorry but I am prepared to take committal before I disclose it."

At this point, the Registrar, Mr E. S. Dobell, interjected to point out to Mr Mitchell and the court that if he refused to answer a question, which he, the Registrar had allowed, he would have to report the matter to the Judge.

Now realising that he had brought the proceedings to a halt, Mr Mitchell, now praying for an adjournment said pompously, "I fully realise the seriousness of my position."

"Let me try again", Mr Dobell said, "You say that you know Mrs Congdon's address?"

Clearly now playing for time Mr Mitchell replied, "I do not say that I know where she is at the present time. I do not know where she is today."

Mr Goodman resumed his question firmly, "I want to know Mrs Congdon's address since she left 16 Victoria Villas, St Budeaux."

"I do not know." Mr Mitchell replied.

"You are aware of some of her addresses Mr Mitchell?" continued Mr Goodman.

"I do not remember."

By this time exasperation was showing on Mr Goodman's face and in his language. "Please do not play with the Court Mr Mitchell." he exclaimed heatedly.

"I am not playing with the Court."

"Do you mean to tell the Court, Mr Mitchell, that you are in a position to get into touch with Mrs Congdon if necessary by letter... is that what you mean?"

"I think that if it is your desire to interrogate her, I think that she is frightened of coming here." Mr Mitchell replied, avoiding answering the question.

"BUNDLE OF NERVES"

He continued seeking sympathy from the court. "The last time I saw Mrs Congdon, she was a bundle of nerves. She told me that Mr Goodman had seen her and scared the life out of her."

Mr Goodman then returned to the questioning. Facing Mr Mitchell he asked. "Had Mrs Congdon told you that on the occasion that I went to St Budeaux to question her, I had not entered the house?"

"No."

"Mr Mitchell, are you in fact asking the court to accept that the explanation for not providing Mrs Congdon's address is that Mrs Congdon has made herself scarce from here because I am alleged to have frightened her?" demanded Mr Goodman.

"Yes," Mr Mitchell replied, "she says you frightened her and her child."

"Are you prepared to disclose Mrs Congdon's address?" Mr Goodman asked.

"I do not know it!" Mr Mitchell replied.

"Then, Mr Mitchell," Mr Goodman announced in a tired voice, "how is Mrs Congdon to be notified that it is desired to interrogate her about these affairs?"

"There are ways of doing it," responded Mr Mitchell.

"DISEASE IN THE HOUSE"

By now the court and court officials were clearly aggravated by Mr Mitchell's procrastination and unwillingness to provide answers. Mr Dobell, the Registrar took over the direction.

"I want to know Mrs Congdon's address, Mr Mitchell!"

"It may be possible," Mr Mitchell said, "to write to certain people, a barrister perhaps who could send out an SOS."

Mr Goodman now resumed his position. "Are you aware, Mr Mitchell, that Mrs Congdon was written to by me asking her to call at my office?"

"No."

"Are you aware," Mr Goodman continued, "that Mrs Congdon said there was infectious disease in the house and intimated that under these circumstances it was undesirable that I should call, or that she should come to see me?"

"No," Mr Mitchell replied.

"Are you aware that it was ascertained that there was no infectious disease notification to the local authority?" asked Mr Goodman.

Mr Mitchell replied that the infection as such was not notifiable. Mr Dobell once more interjected that if Mr Mitchell continued in this way, the court would have no other option than to believe that his obstruction and unhelpfulness were deliberate. That was the only conclusion open to the Court.

Now very much subdued Mr Mitchell announced that the court could communicate with Mrs Congdon care of The GPO (General Post Office) at Kingswood Surrey.

On that announcement, a sense of relief was felt throughout the court and the case moved on. Mr Goodman took his seat and the Registrar signalled that Mr W. L. Broad, of Callington, representing a creditor could ask Mr Mitchell some questions with regard to the administration of Dream Tor and what Mrs Congdon did there. Mr Mitchell described that he worked for Mrs Congdon and earned about one pound per week. When Mr Broad asked what exactly Mrs Congdon's status was, Mr Mitchell replied that she was there in an unofficial position, without salary or reward, it being a mutual agreement that if the place was a success she should expect fair reward for her time and investments. Mr Broad then went on to confirm from Mr Mitchell that Mrs Congdon's position was one of manageress of Dream Tor. Finally wrapping up these questions Mr Broad ventured that surely Mrs Congdon was no longer living on her investment in Dream Tor. Mr Mitchell simply replied that he understood that she was a wealthy woman.

"Did she keep a lot of money in the house?" Mr Broad asked.

"I could not tell you" Mr Mitchell replied, "I have seen Mrs Congdon with £300, even £500 in her purse."

"£500 in her purse, Mr Mitchell?" asked Mr Broad, amazed.
"Yes."

Although the court had not been sitting for long, a key witness, Mrs Congdon, was missing. Mr Dobell considered there was little point in proceeding without her. At that, he adjourned the hearing until July 8th with Mr Mitchell giving an undertaking that he would endeavour to communicate with Mrs Congdon so that she could be at the adjourned hearing.

The game was now clearly up for my mother and father. My father had done his best to protect my mother from the publicity and humiliation of the public court hearing, but the damage was done.

Like it or not, my mother was his willing accomplice. Irene's letter had had the desired impact.

Chapter 9

On The Run

Summer 1938 was hot and sunny as my mother and father contemplated their next move from the comfort of their flat in Maida Vale. All the talk of the time was about Hitler and his expansion plans in Europe, following his annexation of Austria. Prime Minister Neville Chamberlain who had visited Herr Hitler in Bavaria, had come back from Munich waving a piece of paper at the British people saying, "Peace with Honour". The newspapers interpreted this as 'peace in our time'. Despite this, talk of war was very much in the air.

My father's June bankruptcy hearing in Plymouth had been adjourned. Mother's address still remained unknown to the court, although there was now a clear indication that it was somewhere in London. My Father had been careful to post his letters to the court from post boxes all around London, without giving a specific address. This suggested that whilst he may have been in contact with Mrs Congdon, he was not living with her, which was quite untrue. In the meantime, mother and father had garnered their assets, turned them into cash and were considering their next move. The plan for the approaching bankruptcy was that Emanuel would continue to procrastinate and try the court's patience for as long as possible. In a more sober light, and using his experience from numerous court appearances in the Royal Navy, the United States, Canada as well as the Magistrates Court in Plymouth, he quickly reasoned that you could string a Court along; and he did. His form in this respect was verging on the limits of spectacular.

To continue the story as factually as possible, I have again taken the bones of what happened from the newspaper reports of the time and edited them to bring them into focus. Please resume your position in the oak panelled court room as a fly on the wall, but all knowing of the truth.

The case, adjourned from June 3rd, opened again on July 8th 1938. It was a hot summer's day with Plymouth full of visitors enjoying the balmy air blowing off the Hoe. The home fleet was at anchor in Plymouth Sound and the city full of sailors on liberty shore leave. Mr E S Dobell, the Registrar, resumed his position sitting under the Royal Coat of Arms. Mr E S Goodman, the Official Receiver, was ready to continue. The Plymouth Evening Herald journalist once more flipped open his note book ready to report the hearing. Mr Dobell banged his gavel and the court was in session:

Plymouth Evening Herald 8 July 1938

FORMER CITY OSTEOPATH'S NON-APPEARANCE IN BANKRUPTCY COURT
FURTHER ADJOURNMENT OF PUBLIC EXAMINATION DEBTOR SAYS HE IS WITHOUT MONEY FOR RAILWAY FARE

OFFICIAL RECEIVER AND MRS CONGDON

Emmanuel Frederick Mitchell who carried on a practice as an osteopath at the Prudential Buildings, Plymouth, did not appear for his adjourned public examination at Plymouth Bankruptcy Court today, and the examination was further adjourned until August 19. Informing the Registrar that he understood Mr Mitchell would not be present, Mr E S Goodman reminded him that at the former hearing, Mr Mitchell, the debtor, told the Court that he could get in touch with Mrs Congdon, whom it was desirous should be examined in connection with his affairs. He understood that Mr Dobell had received a telephone communication from the lady, as a result of which an appointment was made for her examination in Chambers.

MRS CONGDON'S ADDRESS?

Mr Dobell, continued, "Yes, she telephoned me, saying she understood I wanted to see her and that she would come to Plymouth if I would fix a date. I made the appointment and asked her for her address, but she refused to give it, on the grounds that she was, staying with friends."

Mr Goodman then reminded the court of what had happened. "Subsequent to that conversation, on the day fixed for her private examination I understood that a letter reached you at the Registrar's Office purporting to come from an address at Slough. It stated that for health reasons Mrs Congdon was unable to attend. Based on that information I arranged for inquiries to be made in Slough. I learned that the general address provided by Mrs Congdon was, in fact, a new building estate. There was only one house in that particular area to which her letter referred. My agents were unable to learn that it had any association with Mrs Congdon whatsoever! Nevertheless, in order that there should be no misunderstanding in this matter, I sent a summons to that address for Mrs Congdon to attend court. The date for that examination was yesterday. Mrs Congdon did not appear."

DEBTOR'S POSTCARD

"Without funds to travel to Plymouth"

In some exasperation Mr Goodman continued his presentation to the Court. "It had been my intention, in any event, not to close Mr Mitchell's public examination until I had an opportunity of examining Mrs Congdon's evidence. If Mr Mitchell's examination remained open indefinitely, it was his concern. I wish to remind the court that Mr Mitchell was undoubtedly in a position to get into communication with Mrs Congdon. Furthermore, it would be to his advantage to prevail upon Mrs Congdon to attend for examination. I have to tell the court that this morning I received the following postcard from Mitchell which I shall now read to you:

Dear Sir, - I received your letter and note the remarks about matters over which I have no control. Mrs Congdon was informed by me many weeks ago that the Registrar wished to see her. I conveyed the message as promised, and I cannot do more. I understand that she has had a nervous breakdown.
I have written to the Registrar and stated I am without funds and cannot travel by train or otherwise to Plymouth on July 8. Your attack upon me at the last hearing has prevented me from obtaining employment; therefore I am compelled to ask for the railway fare. Signed EF Mitchell".

THE OFFICIAL RECEIVER'S COMMENT

Having read Mr Mitchell's note to the Court and momentarily paused, Mr Goodman continued. "The answer to that seems to be that if the debtor had the wherewithal to leave Plymouth, there is no reason why, in connection with the investigation of his affairs, he should not return to Plymouth for his examination to be continued."

Mr Dobell remarked, "I received a letter from Mitchell on July 4 last asking if it were possible for his railway fare to be sent to enable him to attend the Court on the 8th. Mr Mitchell said he had no wish to disobey the order of the Court. I replied that there were no funds available for such a purpose. That morning, another letter was received from him stating that he had done everything possible to raise the money for the fare, but without success, and he asked that the examination should be adjourned or concluded in his absence."

HEARING ADJOURNED

Mr Goodman then indicated that there was no chance of the hearing being concluded in Mr Mitchell's absence, on the contrary, that was far too easy an option for Mr Mitchell. "There are other matters intervening and I would like this hearing to be adjourned until August 19th. In the meantime I will communicate with Mitchell at the address he gave. If he is sensible, he will arrange for Mrs Congdon to attend her examination. If everything is straightforward and above-board, as Mr Mitchell suggests, I fail to see what reason there could be for Mrs Congdon avoiding an examination".

Mr Dobell then intervened to ask if there was a medical certificate to account for Mrs Congdon's action and was told there was not. Concluding this hearing, Mr Dobell announced that, "Mr Mitchell must be made to attend the examination. I adjourn the hearing until August 19th".

Evening Herald 19 August 1938

OSTEOPATH ABSENT FROM CITY BANKRUPTCY COURT
REGISTRAR'S COMMENT ON MEDICAL CERTIFICATE

In the continuing Bankruptcy hearing concerning Mr E F Mitchell, an Osteopath of suite 4 & 5 Prudential Buildings, Mr Dobell, the Registrar, read a letter to the Court received from Mr Mitchell's wife, now living in Halifax, Nova Scotia, Canada. He also read out a letter from Mr Mitchell with the address given as Leicester Square, London. It said simply:

"It is regretted that the writer will be unable to attend as directed. Enclosed is a medical certificate informing the reason of inability. Signed: E F Mitchell."

The Medical certificate read,

"I have examined Mr Mitchell and find he has injured his leg and is unable to use it. Signed: Dr J F Penrose."

Mr Dobell continued, "It does not say that he is unable to attend, or unable to travel?"

At this Mr Goodman added. "At the last hearing, the Court received an intimation that Mitchell was unable to attend for financial reasons. In view of that, I arranged for money to be sent to him to purchase the necessary train fare, with some money for incidental expenses for the journey to and from Plymouth, to attend this hearing. He is not here."

FURTHER ADJOURNMENT

Mr Goodman concluded his presentation to the Court by applying for an adjournment until September 16. In his closing remarks he said, "I offer no further comment on his non-attendance. Perhaps by the date suggested the injury to his leg will have improved sufficiently to enable him to attend."

Evening Herald 16 September 1938

DEBTOR AGAIN ABSENT FROM CITY EXAMINATION RECEIVER SAYS CASE WILL BE KEPT OPEN.

When the case of Emmanuel Frederick Mitchell, 41, osteopath, who carried on business at Prudential Buildings, was called for public examination at Plymouth Bankruptcy Court today, a letter was read from him giving as his reason for non-attendance, an injury to his leg. The examination was further adjourned until October 21st, at which date Mitchell hoped to be fit enough to attend. At the outset the Registrar, said that he had received a letter this morning from Mitchell, from an address in Green Street, Leicester Square, London. The Registrar then read the letter.

"IN THE INTERESTS OF JUSTICE"

"With reference to the matter in which I am concerned before you today on the 16th of September, I beg to advise that I am unable to attend, owing to the injury received to my leg. May I further advise that I am unable to wear my boot, the swelling is so bad. I had hoped to be able to attend on the 16th, as there are many matters which I wish personally to present to the Court. I am so informed by medical practitioner and osteopath practitioner that my ankle will take some time before I can get around with comfort. In view of my condition, I respectfully ask you not to allow this case to be closed until I am able to put in my appearance before the Court. In the interests of justice, no doubt you will adjourn the hearing for 30 days. By that time I trust I shall be able to travel with comfort and will be mentally able to answer any questions your department officers may wish. Yours Truly, E F Mitchell."

BEEN IN AN ACCIDENT

Mr Goodman then began his statement to the court, "Mr Mitchell might rest assured the case would not be concluded until he again attended". He then went on to say, "I have not received a medical certificate. However, after the last examination, I have communicated with Mr Mitchell and latterly received a medical certificate. From this exchange it did appear that Mitchell had met with some sort of accident. The doctor who saw him advised Mitchell to have an X-ray examination. It is my opinion that there was some reason for the debtor's non-attendance on the last occasion. However, he had received formal notice of adjournment and was obviously fully cognisant of today's hearing. He is not here. Need more be said?"

Evening Herald 21 October 1938

FORMER PLYMOUTH OSTEOPATH'S LETTERS READ IN COURT REFERENCE TO "COUNTY BASTILLE" FURTHER ADJOURNMENT OF BANKRUPTCY EXAMINATION

Further correspondence from Mitchell, in which mention was made of "application for my committal to the County Bastille" was read at Plymouth Bankruptcy Court today, when the case of Emmanuel Frederick Mitchell, 41, osteopath, who carried on business at the Prudential Buildings was called for public examination. Debtor wrote applying for a further adjournment and stating that his leg was still injured!

Mr Goodman applied to Mr Dobell, the Registrar, for a further adjournment in this case. He said, "If he (Mr Mitchell) is not present then I shall make another application to you."

TO THE OFFICIAL RECEIVER

Addressing the Registrar, Mr Goodman continued. "I have seen the letter Mr Mitchell addressed to the Registrar. This letter I shall now read to the Court:

I have written to the Registrar of Plymouth County Court asking for adjournment to the next sitting of the Bankruptcy Court. I have explained that my leg is still weak and I cannot go far away from the house. My doctor informs me about three weeks' rest and treatment will be necessary and he hopes to discharge me.

I realise lawyers sometimes think that every effort is made by the defendant to delay legal proceedings by excuses, real and fanciful. I can assure you such is not the case. As I recollect I showed you my leg while in your office many months ago and the injury is still present, which I shall be pleased to allow you or anyone to see.

From my past experience with yourself as Official Receiver, I realise you are interested to protect the interest of those who planned my bankruptcy; therefore it maybe your desire to submit the learned Registrar an application for my committal to the County Bastille, pending the disposition of the matter. I have no objection to your submission if such should be the case; only that medical attention shall not be refused me, pending my confinement.

I may say that I do not expect any mercy or sympathy from your hands; however as a member of an honourable profession, you will see justice done to the bankrupt as well as the bank and money lender, Mr Daw." Signed EF Mitchell.

OFFICIAL RECEIVER'S COMMENT

Mr Goodman now spoke to the Court. "In the letter, he had addressed to you, he expressed his willingness, I believe, to be present, but he conveniently omits to put any address on his letter to which communications might be sent. You should know that the letter I have received merely bears a London post-mark with no address. He did give what I presume was an accommodation address in London at another juncture. All my recent communications to that address have been returned with the exception of one which was sent in connection with this examination, and which has not yet been returned. Possibly that will come back in the same way as the others have!"

NO MEDICAL CERTIFICATE

Mr Goodman continued in the same vein, "There is no medical certificate here today. If Mr Mitchell is asking for an adjournment on the grounds of ill-health, the application should be corroborated. By that, I suggest you adjourn the case for one month. If Mr Mitchell is not in attendance, I will ask you to adjourn this bankruptcy case 'sine die' with usual consequences."

Mr Dobell then addressed the court explaining that Mr Mitchell had also written to him. He would now read the letter:

"Dear Sirs,

I should be fit after further rest and treatment after about three weeks. If however, my application for adjournment be granted, I can assure you whatever maybe the condition of my leg, I will make all reasonable efforts to be present. Should this not be satisfactory to the Official Receiver, I am prepared to surrender myself to the nearest police station with the understanding that medical treatment will be accorded me."

Mr Goodman somewhat exasperated spoke to the court. "I say any person honestly desirous of assisting the Court in this matter would not be at such pains to conceal his present whereabouts."

Mr Dobell acknowledged this statement adding, "There was no address on my letter, this case is adjourned until November 18th."

Evening Herald 18 November 1938

FORMER PLYMOUTH OSTEOPATH CRIES AT OFFICIAL RECEIVER
"YOU PERSECUTOR-SHYLOCK, CUT OUT MY HEART"
"PUT ME IN GAOL: I AM NOT GOING TO BE BROWBEATEN BY YOU"
REGISTRAR UPHOLDS MR GOODMAN:
DEBTOR APOLOGISES IN COURT

FINAL EXAMINATION

The official Receiver at Plymouth Bankruptcy Court today concluded his public examination of Emanuel Frederick Mitchell, osteopath, formerly of Plymouth. The case had been adjourned from some months ago. Mr Goodman informed the Registrar, Mr Dobell that as far as he was concerned, the case could be concluded if Mr Mitchell desired to make the necessary application.

Mr Mitchell however refused to make the application for the

closing of the examination, as he declared it might prejudice his intentions of appearing before the County Court Judge on a motion respecting the conduct of the Official Receiver in the case. Consequently, at his request, the examination was adjourned 'sine die' despite the fact that he was informed that the closing would not prejudice any action he desired to take, or that, as an alternative, he might have the examination adjourned generally, which would relieve him of further costs.

This adjourned examination was again marked by several heated exchanges, in the course of which Mr Mitchell alleged that the Official Receiver had been a persecutor and that he had not received fair treatment. At the outset, Mr Goodman desired to put questions relative to what he described as Mr Mitchell's 'American history' and to these Mr Mitchell had objected, claiming that what had occurred in a foreign country, over which this country had no jurisdiction, had no concern with his bankruptcy in this country. The objective, he claimed was based on advice he had received from Crown officers in London.

Mr Dobell spoke clearly to Mr Mitchell "The Official Receiver, Mr Goodman was quite entitled to put questions to you. It is for you to answer them. I will decide whether they were in order."

"WOULD BE NOTED"

"Moreover, you are entitled to confirm or otherwise the replies given on previous occasions, or to vary them if you so desire. This is the function of how this bankruptcy court works. That is why Mr Goodman may question you; to get to the truth, the facts of the matter. It is your duty, Mr Mitchell, to answer the questions put to you. If you decline to answer, then it would be noted."

At this Mr Mitchell continued to protest.

Once more, Mr Goodman addressed the court through direct questions to Mr Mitchell. The first question referred to his alleged deportation from Canada in 1929 and his previous answer that they could not deport him, but instead, he signed an agreement with the Canadian Government for the purpose of repatriation, something very different.

"NOT ORIGINAL DOCUMENT"

Mr Mitchell was asked to examine a copy of a document issued by the Criminal Investigation Department at Ottawa which alleged the deportation of Mr Mitchell as per the steamship, Duchess of York.

Mr Mitchell objected to the document, saying that it was not an original document that he signed in Quebec. "You must be fair", he declared and then added, when the Official Receiver pressed for an answer, "You must not shout me down; I am not going to be browbeaten by you."

Mr Dobell interjected, addressing Mr Mitchell. "Mr Mitchell you are merely being asked whether the statement contained in the document was true or not."

To this the Mr Mitchell replied, "I am not going to say definitely from the document you have produced; it is not an authentic document or an original document from the Canadian authorities."

ADJOURNMENT PLEA

Mr Mitchell continued to be pressed on the question and subsequently said, "I definitely say I signed an agreement to leave Canada to come to this country. If you want to proceed on a charge of perjury, go ahead. What has this to do with my assets?"

Mr Goodman replied quietly, "This is your public examination; I need to ask you any questions relevant to this examination to establish the facts and the truth."

In reply Mr Mitchell asked for an adjournment so that he could go before the County Court, and argue the point of law, and alleged that the Official Receiver was a persecutor! When following this Mr Dobell appealed to Mr Mitchell to listen, Mitchell replied, "I will listen to you because I get a square deal from you. You will not get a square deal from this man because he is a persecutor in the hands of the bank".

DECLINED TO ANSWER

Questions continued to be addressed to Mr Mitchell by Mr Goodman relative to further matters in America.

"Not to my knowledge," Mr Mitchell replied when asked if he had been prosecuted in California in 1916 in the name of Childs.

He further denied that he was prosecuted "for feloniously and with intent to defraud somebody called Learn by a forged cheque."

Mr Mitchell said that he did not remember such an incident.

Mr Mitchell was then questioned relative to five charges of alleged fraud in Los Angeles and to these he replied, "I object to these questions. I protest most strongly. I shall not answer. I wish to inspect and verify all the documentation from which Mr Goodman is reading."

Mr Dobell pointed out that they were not the original documents from which Mr Goodman desired to ask his questions.

At that Mr Mitchell inspected the documents and alleged that they were, "most imperfect."

"JUST UNDERSTAND..."

Mr Dobell now addressed Mr Mitchell in a terse voice saying, "Just understand what you are here for Mr Mitchell."

"I am just here to be persecuted by that gentleman." he said, referring to Mr Goodman.

"That is not so Mr Mitchell." Mr Dobell retorted.

"He has persecuted me and you know it."

Now adopting a strong tone Mr Dobell addressed Mr Mitchell firmly, "You are here to answer your public examination in bankruptcy, to establish the facts."

At that, Mr Mitchell replied fiercely, "I am here to protect my rights. I consider you gave me a square deal, but you never get a square deal from that fellow."

Clearly now exasperated Mr Dobell answered, "Really sir, if it were anybody else I would ask you to take serious notice."

"M. P. WAITING..." (Military Police)

Now realising that he had the stage Mr Mitchell went on. "Quite right; go ahead. Ask the Registrar to commit me to gaol."

Mr Goodman now entered the debate by saying. "I am not going to adopt a course which this gentleman would like very much."

Mr Mitchell now providing a star performance to the court added, "I want you to put me in gaol. There is an M.P. waiting for it. You are a persecutor."

There was a pause as the court regained its dignity and Mr Goodman thought about what to do next. He decided to regain his composure and continue with the basic questions. "Now Mr Mitchell, is it true that in June 1933, you borrowed £250 from a certain lady and gave as security two policies of assurance?"

"Any business I had with the lady had been honourably met."

PROTEST OVER NAME

Mr Goodman continued his questioning. "Did you borrow the money, Mr Mitchell?"

"I know nothing about it. I do not want the name of the woman disclosed."

Mr Dobell now intervened to ask. "Mr Mitchell, this is a perfectly reasonable question. Did you borrow the money and from whom?"

"I am going to object to the question. It is a most improper question. I am going to let you place me in a position to commit me."

Mr Dobell interjected, "You refuse to answer the question, Mr Mitchell."

"I refuse to answer the question."

"BORROWED THOUSANDS"

Continuing with his reply Mr Mitchell went on to say, "I have borrowed thousands of pounds in my time. I do not recollect the transactions of that particular date I don't recollect the transactions of that year. I ask you to make your questions plainer."

Mr Goodman then spoke to the court. "I ask the Court to include in the transcript that Mr Mitchell refuses to name the lady referred to."

"I DON'T REMEMBER"

Mr Mitchell was then questioned by Mr Goodman as to his earlier statement that he purchased Dream Tor, Dousland, for £3,200.

"I have been so ill that I do not remember any statement I made, or what I actually paid."

Mr Goodman continued. "But you do remember buying Dream Tor, Mr Mitchell?"

"I don't remember anything."

Mr Goodman emphasised, "But you remember that, Mr Mitchell?"

"No…. I have been absolutely 'coco' for the past six months. I don't know really what I have been doing. If you have an M.D. here to certify me I think you would be doing the right thing."

Once more Mr Goodman advised Mr Mitchell, "I want you to treat this seriously Mr Mitchell."

"I don't care what you treat. You are a persecutor Shylock, cut out my heart!"

AN APOLOGY

Mr Dobell now addressed Mr Mitchell sternly. "Are you going to behave yourself, Mr Mitchell?"

"I want fair treatment. That man is out to throw mud."

Mr Dobell now anxious to regain control advised Mr Mitchell. "I am not going to have you standing in this court insulting people."

"I will not insult him if you give me a square deal!"

"Will you behave yourself, Mr Mitchell, and apologise for what you have said?" Mr Dobell requested.

After a pause of several seconds and trying to regain his composure, Mr Mitchell replied quietly, "Yes, I am sincerely sorry. Go ahead Mr Goodman."

"RECEIVER'S COMMENTS"

After further questions, which got nowhere, Mr Goodman said if the Registrar liked to close the examination 'well and good', that was fine by him. He went on to say, "I am not going to do certain things which possibly Mr Mitchell would like me to do, for reasons best known to himself. I have gone into the case exhaustively. You can see the type of man he is. If at any future time he should come up for his discharge it will be a matter for me to report to the Court as to his general position, and these other matters which he has objected to answer can be further investigated then. As far as Mrs Congdon (previously mentioned in questions about Dream Tor) is concerned, the closing of the examination will not prevent me taking proceedings with regard to her."

Mr Mitchell was then asked if he wished his examination closed. After prolonged argument the examination was, at his request, adjourned 'sine die'.

****

The hearing had lasted from May until November and still remained unresolved. Emanuel had won, but it was a pyrrhic victory that may have satisfied only his ego. On the Registrar's recommendation, the Judge decided that there was a case to answer and that both my father and mother should go for trial. Accordingly arrest warrants were issued and all assets seized. But, of course, although the court had contacted Emanuel through various accommodation addresses, where in point of fact he and my mother lived was another matter and remained unknown to the court. As the court transcripts testify, my mother never divulged where she was living. Thus, the bolt hole at Clifton Gardens remained undetected for a while. More to the point, save for a few lines in the News of the World, there had been no publicity in the London newspapers. Fright is an awful thing. Fearing the touch on the collar and the indignity of a public arrest, anxiety got the better of both of them. Emanuel's solution was simple; they would go on the run, again. Their money could not last for ever and Emanuel's idle hands and appalling judgement soon took him back to gambling.

From late November 1938, Emanuel and Lenora went on the run living in their caravan as wanted felons. They toured England from Lincolnshire to the Home Counties never staying in one spot too long. This was nothing new for my father, but the effect on my mother was devastating. She now felt the loss of her mother and father, the shame of what had been brought to light and the isolation from her friends and relations. Nobody will ever know how much Emanuel had confided in her about his early life in the US and Canada. I suspect that the revelations about his chequered past made in the bankruptcy court were the first that my mother ever knew or heard. It had a profound effect on her. But it was too late to extricate herself from Emanuel. Never again would she wholly trust him.

Not surprisingly, their relationship now took a nose dive into hostility and a new, more strained and antagonised affiliation. They were inseparable from each other, but only because of their dire circumstances; not because of happiness, love and contentment. My mother, ever the realist, saw the future with fear and foreboding and without support. Their money was haemorrhaging at an alarming rate. To make matters worse, she rowed constantly with Emanuel demanding that he obtain some form of employment to help with the bills. The last thing they wanted, she said, was to draw attention to themselves as a result of unpaid bills. She had repeatedly told him that unpaid bills were a certain way back to jail. But how could Emanuel work? He was a wanted man for a whole string of offences dating back to the Royal Navy and now bankruptcy. To cap it all he had no papers.

By the late spring of 1939 after touring England in their caravan mother and father considered it safe to return to the flat in Maida Vale. They had patched up their differences and in an uneasy peace and tolerance, decided to remain together for mutual support. Emanuel would do what he could to find work, but it would take time. As the grey, war clouds gathered over England in the summer of 1939, London County Council, fearing the worst, passed legislation for the construction of air raid shelters all over the capital. Appeasement, as the newspapers called it, was clearly not going to work with Herr Hitler. London needed to be prepared. In order to staff the new civil defence organisation, interviews had begun to identify potential managers who were outside of call-up age and who might be able to undertake supervisory or managerial responsibilities.

Whilst thumbing through the Star Newspaper, Emanuel spotted an advertisement, tore out the page and decided to see what he could do. To put inquisitive noses off his rather strong scent, he could always revert to being Scottish, American or Canadian. It had certainly worked in the past. Here was a chance for him to be useful and to get on the pay roll again. He would now try and re-invent himself and gain managerial employment with London County Council dropping any illusion to his medical past and quack qualifications. From London County Council's point of view he seemed ideally qualified to work within their survival and recovery plans. The whole organisation was entitled Civil Defence. Within this framework came Air Raid Precautions (ARP). As a sub organisation, war time only, under ARP came something described as the Rest Centre Service. It was to be within this organisation that my father would have another chance.

Notes.

Sine Die is Latin for 'without day' a legal term. . When the court or other body rise at the end of a session or term they adjourn sine die. In layman's terms the case remains open and can re-commence at any time. Dream Tor was virtually wholly destroyed in the fire and was eventually demolished. The site has never been re-built and is now a garden. The carriage house and stables remain. The railway station for Dousland is now a private residence and the railway track just a scar on the landscape. During the blitz on Plymouth many of the court records were destroyed, or if they remained were destroyed under the thirty year rule later on. The only reliable records come from the court transcripts printed in the local papers, The Western Morning News, Plymouth Evening Herald and finally The Tavistock Times. The arrest warrants, although issued, were never acted upon. The war of 1939–45 overtook everything.

Chapter 10

The end of the Dream

On September 3rd, 1939, nearly ten years after Emanuel had returned to the UK from Canada, he sat down together with his new family of Lenora and Thelma in their flat in Maida Vale to listen to the 11 am broadcast given by the Prime Minister. It was a lovely September day. A breeze passed through the open French doors of their third floor flat allowing the curtains to flutter gently. At last the chimes of Big Ben were heard and then Mr Chamberlain announced that he was speaking to the nation from the Cabinet Rooms of 10 Downing Street. "This morning the British Ambassador in Berlin handed the German Government a final note stating that unless the British Government heard from them by 11 o'clock, that they were prepared at once to withdraw their troops from Poland, a state of war would exist between us. I have to tell you now that no such undertaking has been received and that consequently this country is at war with Germany." Shortly after this, the air raid siren sounded for the first time. It was a false alert.

In the fog of threats that preceded this announcement mobilisation had already begun to some extent. Now it would happen in earnest. At age forty-three Emanuel knew that he would not be called up for military service, but he would be liable for local government work. There was no such thing as 'the unemployed' in wartime. Sadly, he would never again be able to use his gift and ability as an osteopath as he knew that the moment he divulged that information, checks would be made and his cover, such as it was, would be blown. Although, ostensibly he and mother appeared to live together at various addresses, the truth was that from time to time Emanuel would simply disappear, involved in one scam or another and my mother became increasingly stressed and harassed by his behaviour. His hunger for gambling and women had also taken its toll on the money the pair had accrued after the Dream Tor. By the start of the WW2, funds were becoming so scarce that, "doing a flit" as it was called, became the order of the day when the rent could not be paid.

After hastily leaving Maida Vale, mother was called up for service to drive an ambulance, as part of the national mobilisation programme. Nothing very much happened so she was released and found a position with accommodation as an auxiliary nurse at Long Grove Mental Hospital in Surrey. Emanuel, on the other hand, received a reply to his application and joined the ranks of the London County Council Rest Centre Service. This division of Civil Defence was set up to provide emergency support if and when the bombing started. Thelma was sent back to Devon in the hope that by staying with her grandparents in Bridestowe she would be at low risk from aerial bombing attacks. In the meantime, 'the phoney war', as it was called, continued with neither side prepared to move from their entrenched positions; at least not quite yet.

In the March 1940 edition of The London Gazette my father was officially made bankrupt at last bringing a closure to the case. According to the Bailiff's ledger, there were few assets to be recovered from his consulting rooms in Prudential Buildings. His only other asset of value was the freehold of the land on which Dream Tor stood. This was valued at £300. In due course the land was sold through the offices of Mr Goodman so my father's creditors did, at least, receive something.

On May 10th 1940, Winston Churchill became Prime Minister. During the same month Belgium, Holland and France fell to the advancing German Army leaving the British Expeditionary Force to be evacuated from Dunkirk. In June the Italians declared war against Britain and in July the Battle of Britain began, culminating in the air raids on London and other major cities. After a brief stint at Long Grove Hospital, mother moved on to a boarding School in Chislehurst, to become a matron where Thelma could join her for a while. These were the closing days of the summer of 1940 when Thelma watched aircraft weaving vapour trails over the South Downs during the 'dog fights' of The Battle of Britain. Meanwhile, my father had completed his training and had joined the Rest Centre Organisation. My mother, on the other hand joined the staff of British Restaurants, quickly rising to become a manageress. These were state organised collective feeding centres where by pooling rations, meals were kept at a low price. They proved to be very successful and even popular, although some of the dishes involving whale meat, like Snook, were less appetising and the source of great ridicule.

Now in full employment with wages coming in from two sides my father and mother settled down in an uneasy relationship. For a while, they were able to leave their troubles behind as they became wholly engrossed in their work. My mother opened facilities at Farnborough, and Aldershot and took lodgings close by. Emanuel visited from time to time. Once more life was on the up for them. Emanuel was promoted to become an area supervisor in the much destroyed Camberwell area of South London. Later on, he was asked to include the neighbouring Balham area of London. The work was demanding and he appeared to rise to the challenge. The air raids on South London had been particularly heavy and many acres of housing had been destroyed leaving countless people homeless. For whatever reason, perhaps a sense of purpose, perhaps just a sense of responsibility, the relationship with my mother calmed and once more they decided to live together and try again as a couple. In 1941 they moved into a rented seven bedroom Edwardian Town House in Herne Hill, South London. To keep matters above board, given that my father and mother had different surnames, Emanuel was introduced to the neighbours as my mother's brother. Quite what the neighbours thought when the children began arriving is not recorded. My mother, ever the effective business woman, at once saw the opportunity to rent out the extra bedrooms to lodgers in an accommodation strapped London. From 1941 onwards, she ceased working and commenced to have Emanuel's offspring. My sister Susan was born in 1942, my brother Peter in 1944 and myself in 1946. Throughout the war years my father's lust for life and excitement seemed to know no bounds along with his passion for womanising and gambling particularly at the dog tracks.

In July 1944, the V weapon, 'doodle bug' missile attacks began against London. Once more my father came into his own, dealing with the displaced and homeless. Minutes after leaving a rest centre in Balham the building he had just inspected took a direct hit from a V 2 rocket. He was lucky. The anomaly with this weapon was that the sound of the rocket approaching was heard after the explosion, since the speed of the rocket was greater than that of sound itself. At home in Herne Hill, mother and Susan were caught when a V1 landed opposite the house, causing the front elevation to blow-in. Although mother remained only shaken, Susan had to be rescued from under the debris as the ceiling had collapsed on to her cot. On May 8th, 1945 the European war ended. As a matter of adjustment, the Rest Centre Service slowly ran down, handing over its responsibilities to peace time council officials. Within months, my father found himself unemployed. He took it badly. He very much enjoyed his work, the routine, the team spirit, the companionship with others and possibly most of all being recognised and valued. He hoped that the Council might renew his employment in another sphere. It was a forlorn hope. There were now thousands coming back from the war to be de-mobilised and who would want work. He was fifty and priority would have to be given to younger men. Emanuel fell into depression. At his age, he had little hope of achieving well paid work despite the recommendations he had received during the war. His weaknesses got the better of him and he turned to any scam that he thought could make him money.

The last known photo circa 1946

Gambling headed the list. This was a repeat of the same pathetic hope that he had expressed when writing to Irene about buying a ticket in the Irish Sweepstake in 1934. Just one good bet and everything would be fine. He was hooked and it would always be the next race or the race after that, or a feeling of luck, or a tip, or just intuition. There is nothing a desperate man will not do if he believes; and Emanuel would always believe that sometime his luck would come home. His gambling became an obsession. He hoped that perhaps he could buy back the affection of those he loved and restore his dignity. But it wasn't to be. He took up some casual work, but he was now a shadow of his former self. For a while he lived in at the Ship Hotel, Brighton where he worked as a door man and later moved to the Strand Palace hotel in London. Curiously, in March 1946, when my father recorded my birth he insisted on including the name Mitchell on the certificate and gave his occupation as a 'maintenance engineer' or more probably odd job man at one of the London hotels.

By early 1948, the relationship between my parents was so bad that fights and physical harm were frequent between them. At the same time my father was becoming increasing ill with kidney associated problems. By the summer, he had been in and out of hospital several times and was now bed-ridden at home with Thelma undertaking most of the care. Despite these circumstances, the relationship with my mother remained strained and unforgiving. Her hate and dislike for him had reached new levels as more and more revelations came to the surface. Over the preceding eighteen months, to feed his gambling habit, he had taken mother's jewellery and valuable possessions, her last connection with her home and parents, and pawned them. To make matters worse and as no surprise to the reader, all the money raised was lost at the dog track. But that was not the end of the story. There were strange visitors to the house, 'associates' of his bearing IOUs that required urgent redemption. There were letters from a probation officer that suggested that he had again made an appearance in court and had been found guilty. Finally, to cap it all, Thelma discovered that jewellery given to her as a child had been pawned and lost by him.

On July 18th 1948, four days before his fifty-second birthday, my father died quietly and sadly of 'chronic nephritis', so Doctor Roberts wrote on his death certificate. On the same certificate my mother recorded herself as, 'L Congdon Mitchell', widow of the deceased! On July 22nd, my father's birthday, he was buried without fuss in Norwood cemetery, South London. Although it was not a pauper's funeral, there is no stone to remember him, just a grid reference on the cemetery plan. The man who would be king of his own making was now gone. The only person to attend the funeral from my father's family was his older sister, Mary with whom he had somehow maintained contact. She was never seen or heard of again. But what on earth was nephritis?

When I joined the RAF and declared that my father died of nephritis, it was accepted without comment. Whenever I asked those of the medical profession what actually it was I was always left with a vague stare and 'inflammation of the kidneys'. When I asked if there were any long term complications or hereditary implications, I was assured, 'no!' But of course there was more to this ailment, much, much more.

Nephritis seems to have been a disease of war. In terms of magnitude, in 1917, it was recorded as affecting more than 15,000 soldiers. (It was a huge military liability. Only frostbite with 21,000 casualties and venereal disease with 48,000 accounted for more hospital admissions.) However, most sufferers got over their initial infection (or thought they did) after prolonged rest and treatment. It was an odd, illogical almost intangible illness. The malady insidiously crept up on the casualty over a period of weeks, sometimes months. It often began with breathlessness, headaches, coughing a night, pains in the limbs and chest, and vomiting. There followed heavy sweats and weight loss which could, in extreme circumstances, be as much as five pounds over 24 hours. The repercussions included an enlarged heart (which was true of my father) with the potential to cause a cerebral haemorrhage (possibly the cause of his death). But as to what actually this illness was or what caused it remained obscure until the post war years.

In WW1 nephritis was attributed to the atrocious conditions that existed in the trenches. The source of infection was tracked down to vermin and lice. There were so many unattended dead bodies on the battlefields of France that rats proliferated as never before. Rat and human urine was everywhere aggravated by excrement leaching into the ground water. Today this infection of ordure is associated with lupus. There is a suggestion (important for the descendents to know) that there could be some hereditary implications with this infection, although investigations are vague at the moment. Like many illnesses, nephritis can lie dormant for several years, as was the case with my father, only to flair up in later life when earlier conditions under which the illness prospered are repeated, or simply the body resistance is weak. The next question had to be how did my father come into contact with this infection?

Like most WW1 soldiers, other than in general terms to my sister Thelma, my father did not talk much about his war experiences. As a battlefield "medic" the awful carnage and dreadful casualties that he must have seen would have left a frightening impression. He would not wish to rekindle these memories in conversation. This is, of course, the basis of what we now understand as post traumatic stress. The mind has somehow to come to terms with these often recurrent, awful memories. The best way of doing this may be not to talk about them and to let "sleeping dogs lie". So once more it is necessary to piece together a circumstantial cause. Although there is no conclusive evidence, my father would likely have spent brief periods away from the casualty ships, in the trenches at casualty clearing stations. There is no doubt that many of the casualties that he handled, touched, washed or wound-dressed would have been in a filthy state potentially carrying the nephritis infection.

In the last years of his life, during various periods of estrangement from my mother, my father lived where he could, conceivably even as a vagrant. According to my sister, after the war he was often to be seen in dishevelled state. Perhaps this experience and his living conditions once more reproduced the circumstances necessary for nephritis to strike again? In July 1948 it would be the final coup de grâce. Above all, the mere fact that he had this disease and that at the end it claimed him gives a strong image of the hard and unforgiving life that he led.

In a story entitled, "Journey to my father" his death might seem the right place to bring matters to a close. But the repercussions of his relationship with my mother were to run on. Emanuel died without a will and certainly no estate. He left no tangible memento to his three children by Lenora or indeed to his four children by Irene, now growing up in the United States and who were totally oblivious to what had happened in England. To the American family, Emanuel Frederick was a painful memory to his children, David and Jennie, a ghost memory to Gordon and nobody to Ronald. He would always be the father who abandoned them; a silver tongued trickster and serial philanderer, a con man. He was universally disliked, if not despised; all with good cause.

For my mother, now a single parent with three children, no employment and living on the rents coming in from unused rooms in the house, every day was a trial. Emanuel had left only debts. Thelma now worked skivvying at home, cooking and cleaning the lodgers' rooms after completing her daytime job at the bank, all to help the family's solvency. The future in 'Austerity Britain' looked grim.

Providence was now to take a hand in our lives which would give my mother the opportunity to secure a future for us all. In the late autumn of 1947, my grandfather, Sidney John, died intestate. As the law then prescribed, a portion of her father's estate had to be given to my mother as well as the residue going to his widow, Elizabeth. Two things now happened: mother received a much needed cash injection from her father's estate and she was now in contact with her mother. Up until this time Elizabeth Kate had been totally unaware of the children her daughter had given birth to during the wartime years. As mother announced and then displayed her instant family, Elizabeth's pretensions to strict Methodism must have been sorely tested. "What would the people think in Bridestowe" – which indeed became our problem in later life when, as children, we visited the village. People gazed at us with almost open mouths, "so that's them!" Eventually our grandmother came to live with us until her own demise in the winter of 1954, when mother gained her full inheritance.

My mother continued to use her legal married name of Congdon after Emanuel's death. Susan and Peter, aged six and four at the time of our father's death assumed that the kindly middle-aged man of whom they had a vague recollection, was in fact Harry Congdon: an easy deception. Mother never disabused them of this notion. The next thought in her mind was to remove all possible reference to the Mitchell name by anecdote or on paper. The paper could be dealt with easily by providing us all with shortened birth certificates that contained only the barest details, certainly nothing about our father. To remove the anecdotal evidence would mean somehow muzzling Thelma. She was the only one, so mother thought who could spill the beans about her previous life.

In 1955 Thelma married for a second time and was suddenly gone from our lives. We children were told never to contact her again.

The discovery and extent of Emanuel's American family was not to come until fifty one years later in 2006. Thelma had an inkling that Emanuel had a connection with someone called Irene from a photo that she remembered seeing on the wall in Emanuel's consulting rooms in Prudential Buildings, Plymouth. Later she remembered that when the song 'Goodnight Irene' was played on the Radio, mother would turn the radio off announcing how she disliked that name. Emanuel had also regaled Thelma with stories from his American past, his life in Hollywood, but he never talked of a wife and children.

My mother went peacefully to her grave in 1984 with all her secrets. She was buried in the same churchyard as her father and mother in Bridestowe. She gained a divorce from Henry (Harry) Congdon in 1957 and later re-married in the 1970s. It was not until 2006, when I received a copy of father's photograph taken in San Quentin prison, complete with number across his chest, that I realised what a strong likeness I bore to him, and how much this must have disturbed my mother. In my boyhood and early years, when the pain and anguish of her relationship with Emanuel was still a strong memory and maybe a powerful feeling, perhaps I had become the reincarnation of the devil; the man who had brought her so much unhappiness, misery and distress?

Chapter 11

Epilogue

When I set out on this journey I had no idea what I would find, least of all three half-brothers and a half-sister in the United States. Secretly, I hoped that I would discover a father hero figure that I could look up to and someone who would offer credibility in conversation. But that was not to be. As I perused the historic records, the detail of my father's life became clear. I was initially ashamed and then angry that one man could create so much misery and destroy so many lives by his selfishness. There was also the knock-on effect which affected mine and I believe so many other lives on both sides of the Atlantic. Then I began a realisation that I must be honest with myself. I did not want to admit it, but I began to recognise so much of myself in this man. There were so many parallels. He took up farm work to escape the workhouse. I took up farm work to escape home life. Bored with farm work he joined the Navy. Seeing no future in farm work I joined the RAF. I now realise that we are born with certain traits that only life and the influence of others can either straighten out, or compound. My father had a dim view of authority and so did I. My father was a self starter, so was I. The similarities go on. But I was lucky; I had mentors who endeavoured to set me on the right path when I strayed.

For what my mother suffered and Irene before her at Emanuel's hands, I have only passionate sympathy. My own relationship with my mother was extremely difficult until the last months of her life thanks to my dislike and almost hatred of her for her treatment of my older sister and myself. Now I know the whole story. I cannot condone what she did to Thelma, but in a way, I understand why she did it as a form of protection for us all. My full sister and brother were more malleable than myself and found it easy to accept mother's domineering ways and for the most part enjoyed a good relationship with her throughout her life. My mother was an adventurous woman who fell under the spell of a confidence trickster, serial philanderer and petty crook. She never really recovered from taking him into her life, always having to look over her shoulder wondering who might tell or say something. After Emanuel's death she did what she could to bring up three children, single-handed in the tired austerity years after WW2. Like Irene, my mother worked hard all hours to feed, clothe and hold us together as a family. In a way this book is an apology to her, from me and also to put her side of the story as one of Emanuel's many, perhaps countless victims.

What do I think now of my father? It is difficult for me to look at him objectively. All the records filed about him relate to a con artist, a consummate actor and possible arsonist, with Walter Mitty tendencies and more. He was not driven by alcohol, although he understood its value and capitalised on it during prohibition, if only to survive. On the personal side he certainly had an inexhaustible appetite for sex and adventure, but with an appalling judgement and sense of responsibility. He preferred female company to male and seems not to have had long term friends beyond Irene and my mother. I have found no references to male friends close or otherwise. The conclusion must be that he was a loner. In other circumstances he may have prospered as a bright, possibly gifted child with a deep interest in medicine. He was certainly a self motivated go-getter, but sadly missed the example of a father, or a relation, or friend even who could act as a mentor to keep him on track. The workhouse has much to answer for.

Most children these days are over managed by their parents who see them through life, sometimes into their early twenties, often much later. Emanuel was on his own from a babe in arms. He was a product of a flawed institutional life style that had the best of intentions. Whatever happened to him in the Royal Navy to cause him ultimately to desert remains a profound mystery; we can only guess. As a young, attractive boy I have a hidden fear that he may have become prey for the sexual extremes of one of his mess mates. Sadly, the reputation for buggery in the Navy was well known, if ignored. His response and reaction to what happened is so dramatic and extreme that it had to be something that he could neither relate to, nor willingly accept as part of life. Had young Emanuel been unwilling to participate, then it is more than probable that he would have been bullied and picked on until he did accept the situation. He was, after all, an immature, sixteen years old at the time, perhaps to "them" a virgin! Moreover the conditions on HMS New Zealand, at Esquimalt and on HMS Algerine and Shearwater, his final posting, were unlikely to stimulate a bright lad. Maybe, his only option to get away from the closed mess society below deck was to desert. He was certainly ill prepared when he made his escape as is illustrated by what happened in San Diego. When cast adrift, he made a complete dog's breakfast of managing his life, ending up once more behind bars, but behind bars that protected and fed him.

On his release, he tries hard to overcome the past and start again. He signs up first for the US Army and then for the Canadian Army. He does well reaching the rank of sergeant. He is motivated by medicine and seems to have mentors amongst the doctors who take an interest in him. All too soon, however, the war is over and his mentors gone and his girl is pregnant. After WW1 and marriage he knows what he wants, but for want of sensible counsel and financial help, he fails, turning to petty crime in the US and Canada to fund his studies and family. Finally, he is repatriated to his country of birth. But he is a survivor with a taste for excitement, women and gambling. He tries again in England and begins to make steady progress, but upsets the establishment by his observations; and his wife by womanising.

One outstanding question regarding his later life remains. How bad was the leg and knee injury he reported to the Canadian authorities and which, supposedly, later kept him from attending the Plymouth bankruptcy court? Was it all bullshit and procrastination? The answer is that in later life his left leg did show signs of degeneration and severe ulceration. Was this caused by an accident in a 1911 football match; was his knee cap wired? That remains unclear. He did suffer knee pain during his Oakalla prison term and was seen and x-rayed for knee damage that described the symptom as "weeping" which was the same description used by the Halifax NS hospital in 1919. The conclusion must be that he did have a real knee and leg problem that was compounded over time and included a circulatory problem in later mid life. The answer is revealed when he died. The doctor records nephritis on his death certificate. That was the progressive 'cross' he had to bear. He would have seen it in others and no doubt noted the symptoms, but as so often happens to doctors, they fail to recognise symptoms in themselves. This was in fact the case of my brother Peter who sadly died of cancer. Although himself a doctor, he seemed blind to the symptoms he experienced.

Of course, my father's life was not all failure. He clearly felt some sense of duty and responsibility for the women who had suffered profound emotional loss at the Plymouth maternity home. Were it not for him calling the Plymouth medical establishment to account regarding puerperal fever, the 1933 court case would never have happened. That being the case he could have had a happy and successful life as an osteopath in the West of England until his death. How cruel fate was to him. Instead, big ideas got the better of him and he went off the rails, again. Emanuel was a risk taker with sadly poor judgement. He probably did burn down Dream Tor for the insurance money, but I doubt my mother was wholly in on the plan. His conduct during the bankruptcy hearing verged at times on the comic, but showed a very intelligent man playing the system for all its worth. Yes, the war saved him again and he had another chance. He had some success with the London County Council rest centre service, but once the war was over, the gambling bug got him and destroyed his relationship with my mother. To cap it all, the kidney illness that today would be curable became the cause of his death. As cruel as it may sound, perhaps his death was a blessing to us all. In the years that followed, the families on both sides of the Atlantic tried to discover more about Emanuel and what happened to him. The rumour in America was that he died in England during WW2. The American family then tried to trace him through his so called Scottish ancestry; he was, after all, Scottish to them. Unsurprisingly, that drew a blank. No records existed for a Scottish Emanuel Mitchell. At that point there was nothing more the American family could do.

There is a second story within this tale that has not yet been written. It is what happened to Irene when she returned to Nova Scotia on the RMS Ascania. From the investigations so far undertaken there is good evidence that during her stay in Treville Street, Irene was aware of Emanuel's dalliance with my mother. Perhaps it was the last straw and the action that drove her to want to return to Canada, albeit that she was carrying Emanuel's child. Certainly when she left in 1933 there was only ever a single ticket. On her arrival in Halifax, far from the welcome she dreamed of, she was shunned. She was rejected by her family and had no option but to put her children in care whilst she was confined to give birth to Ronald. Once Ronald was born she removed the children from care and thereafter brought up the four children single handed, finally settling in the United States. It was a miraculous tale of self-sacrifice for her children. Despite her good looks and charm, she never involved herself with a man again. Apart from just a few utterances, she took all her secrets to her grave. Her inner strength was remarkable.

David, Jennie, Gordon and Ronald, my half-brothers and half-sister, all thrived in their own right becoming successful: David became an accomplished self-made engineer and entrepreneur, Gordon a renal consultant at Walter Reed Hospital, Ronald a first sergeant in the US Army who saw active service in the Korean War and like my full brother tragically died young. What happened to Irene Jane is less known. Like her mother she was extremely attractive and married twice. Three strands seem to flow through the family covering an interest in medicine, military matters and engineering.

Perhaps by coincidence, the same strands are evident in the family that Emanuel sired in England. My brother became a consultant paediatrician, my sister, a self-starter hotelier with her husband. I enjoyed a military career with a strong interest in engineering. More to the point, the same strands continue today in the American family where some of the nephews have followed those same paths. As for Thelma, against all the odds, her resilience took her into two marriages and a hugely successful career in London as an entrepreneur, eventually becoming a Freeman of the City of London, a rare achievement. What happened on both sides of the Atlantic is all the more remarkable as both Irene and Lenora had to bring up families single handed with virtually no welfare support.

What happened to me? In many ways I was my father's son. I have some sympathy for my father whom I think was let down by the system on board HMS New Zealand. Yes, I got the job following the interview and for the most part enjoyed the rest of my military service. However, in 1987 my military career came to a crisis point. I was ordered to undertake recruit training with firearms and live ammunition that I knew to be dangerous, well beyond the limits of recognised and accepted safety. I refused to give the orders to my subordinate instructors. In so doing I believed that the 'system' would back me up. It did not. (That was my HMS New Zealand.) As far as the 'system' was concerned, I had refused to obey an order of a superior officer. Just as in my father's tussle with the establishment in 1933, (another parallel,) nobody was interested in the defining issue of safety. The point was how dare I question "The Establishment". Ranks of the smart and bum licking closed against me with a most unhealthy rapidity. All of a sudden I found that I had no friends and life was made unbearable through isolation. I resigned from the service by seeking early retirement. An earlier parachuting injury was also now making its mark felt. What followed was what they now call 'post traumatic stress '. In short, I felt ill and betrayed. I found it difficult to reason and come to terms with why the establishment let me down. For a while, like my father, I drifted in employment and nearly destroyed my marriage. A year later I moved to British Aerospace to re-invent myself working within a department called Operations Development.

Following the invasion of Iraq, with the Prime Minister's agreement I lead a joint military/civil training team to Saudi Arabia to train the Saudi Armed Forces in the skills of post nuclear, biological and chemical attack. It was a huge success and earned British Aerospace and the UK Government both kudos and millions of pounds in profit. For my trouble I was awarded a war medal and a company commendation. But as the war clouds unfolded and time became critical, I found that the company were cheating on their employees by withholding essential, protective equipment. Once more I stood up, once more the ranks of the company directors closed against me. I had been let down again. But somehow, nothing surprised me anymore. After that, just like my father, I had to re-invent myself. This time I returned to Saudi Arabia and took up appointments in Bahrain and Saudi Arabia as an independent defence consultant and life was much more rewarding. For the rest of my working life I remained as a specialist defence consultant working for UK industry and clients in the Gulf countries, before the parachuting injury and kidney problems finally made long term work impossible. I retired to France for the climate and life style. As the reader will note, the traits within ancestry often repeat themselves, but never quite exactly.

It is important to know where you come from and what your true identity is in order to understand yourself. Whether we like it or not, we inherit both looks and traits from our ancestors. Depending on which route we take in life these gifts, and I use that word with emphasis, can be for good or bad. Now at age 64, I can lay the ghosts of the past to rest, knowing the truth. Most of all, I have now come to know myself.

It is the great tragedy of my life that all my half-brothers and sister in America died before I found them in the year 2007. It is probably too late to form other than a superficial relationship with my American family now, but I have made a start and cherish the new contacts.

As has so often been said to me, "You can choose your friends, but not your family".

The final irony to this story was revealed in 2010 and relates back to that desire one has to have family pride and to know where you come from. You will recall that my grandmother died in penury in 1898. Her maiden name was Letton. Thanks to Ancestry.com we can now trace this family name back to the de Medici family on one side and Queen Matilda of England on the other. That is true irony. It is also true life.